FOR THE
COMMON
GOOD

Participant Handbook

ED O'MALLEY

JULIA FABRIS MCBRIDE

AMY NICHOLS

KLC Press
Kansas Leadership Center
325 East Douglas, Wichita, Kansas, USA, 67202

Visit our website at *www.kansasleadershipcenter.org*

This edition published in 2014

ISBN: 978-0-9889777-3-0

Cover designed by Clare McClaren, Novella Brandhouse
Book design by Patrick Hackenberg

Printed in the United States of America

This book is dedicated to:

Ed O'Malley, Sr.,
whose well-worn Marine Corps Handbook
was the inspiration for this book

and

Marty Linsky,
our teacher and friend.

Table of Contents

Section I: Preparing for the Experience

Section II: In the Experience

Section III: Onward!

Acknowledgments

Although three authors are officially listed on the front of this handbook, countless people have contributed to the ideas it contains. We are thankful to the staff, faculty, coaches and consultants of the Kansas Leadership Center who have experimented with several iterations of this material and improved it along the way.

Marty Linsky, Ron Heifetz and Cambridge Leadership Associates have been key partners for seven years, especially helping us explore the nature of adaptive challenges and the use of Case-in-Point teaching. The voice of David Chrislip, co-author of our first book — *For the Common Good: Redefining Civic Leadership* — is also present throughout this handbook.

Greg Meissen worked with Ed to develop the first version of the "Playbook" (chapter 7.) Without Greg's imagination and dedication then, we wouldn't be at this point now.

We are thankful to the members of the Kansas Leadership Center board of directors. Their visionary and supportive style has enabled KLC to thrive.

None of this — the idea of KLC, let alone this handbook — would be possible without the far-sighted leadership of the Kansas Health Foundation, which in 2006 decided a statewide center to develop leadership for the common good was and forever would be essential.

Finally, we are indebted to the thousands of participants who have engaged with our team. The ideas in this handbook have been strengthened by them and through them.

Introduction

If you are reading this, you are likely someone who cares about moving your organization, company, neighborhood, family, community, state or nation forward. You have decided to explore ideas to help you make more progress on things you care most about. Congratulations!

We say "congratulations" because most people never take this step. They never deliberately explore how to improve their effectiveness. They just exist. They might do good things, or they might not. But what does or doesn't happen isn't about them; in their minds, it's about everyone and everything else.

It takes a motivated, self-discerning individual to journey to greater self-discovery and mastery. You're on that journey, and we're excited to be with you. You'll benefit, but more importantly, you'll advance the common good around you.

This book is an aid, not the complete picture. It is designed to work in concert with your *For the Common Good* program. You'll notice many pages don't make sense without explanation from a coach, faculty or staff member of our organization. Don't worry; everything will be explained in time. Of course, if you have questions or curiosities now, contact us and we'll walk you through whatever is on your mind.

Included here are resources, explanations, charts, tables, information and ideas that you and your fellow participants will explore thoroughly during your program experience. Depending on the program, some of the things in this book may or may not be utilized, but by the end of the experience, it will be an ongoing resource for your development and learning.

The book is organized into three sections. Section I readies you for the *For the Common Good* experience. You'll read an overview of different learning methods we utilize and prepare the leadership challenge you wish to work on during your experience. You should read and complete Section I before beginning your program.

Section II is a playbook of sorts for your leadership challenge. We'll help you better understand your challenge and plot ways forward. By the end of your experience, this section will contain your notes, scribbles, ideas, 'aha moments,' etc. Section II doesn't make much sense without a member of our team's facilitation. We wouldn't advise digging into this section much before your experience.

Section III looks past your *For the Common Good* program experience and describes more ways to understand the ideas presented during your experience.

It's not needed to prepare for your program, but you might be interested in perusing some of our other resources, including:

- *For the Common Good: Redefining Civic Leadership,* co-authored by Ed O'Malley and David Chrislip (author of *The Collaborative Leadership Fieldbook*). David and Ed tell the story of the Kansas Leadership Center and assert that leadership must become more purposeful, engaging and provocative if we are to make progress on society's daunting challenges.

- *For the Common Good: Teaching Guide,* co-authored by Chris Green and Julia Fabris McBride. This book is great for anyone interested in our methods of instruction: Case-in-Point, case studies and coaching. (Coming soon from KLC Press)

- *Your Leadership Edge:* co-authored by Ed O'Malley and Amanda Cebula, this book breaks down the *For the Common Good* principles and competencies. With specific advice on how to do things like raise the heat, speak to loss, give the work back, etc., this book is a tremendous resource for anyone trying to put the *For the Common Good* ideas into action.

- *The Journal,* published by the Kansas Leadership Center each quarter, is packed full of stories about people exercising the type of leadership we desperately need more of in our world. *www.kansasleadershipcenter.org/thejournal*

In the first paragraph of this introduction, we made one assumption about your motivation. Now we'll make another. Chances are you believe, at some level, we all share responsibility for acting together in pursuit of progress. You're not alone in that belief. It's been important in Kansas Leadership Center experiences since our start in 2007.

The sentiment captured in the phrase *For the Common Good* is grounded in the thoughts and feelings of those who walked this path before you.

For the Common Good is reflective of our collective hope of the work upon which you're about to embark.

Onward!

SECTION I

Preparing for the Experience

CHAPTER 1

Leadership and the Common Good

It's not leadership if it's not for the common good.

Leadership is mobilizing others to make progress on deep, daunting, "adaptive" challenges. Those adaptive challenges are concerns facing our companies and communities that are crying out for more leadership but seldom get it. Why is leadership elusive?

1. **It's hard to define the problem, let alone discover a solution.** Trying to define tough problems in detail can ignite controversy. Is global warming a natural occurrence or man-made catastrophe? Is loss of market share the result of ineffective marketing or lack of company innovation? Is poor school performance due to changes in parenting or static teaching models?

2. **People would rather not be bothered by daunting challenges.** They would rather assume someone else, someplace else is dealing with it. Putting off work on issues like long-term viability of Social Security is an example. Another example is lack of succession planning in a business.

3. **It's risky.** People don't like it when you try to get them to do things they would rather not. You'll become a target.

4. **We mesh leadership and management/authority into the same thing, thus placing too much burden on those with authority and too little expectation on those without.**

5. **It requires engaging lots of people.** We are groomed to think leadership is about being the smart one with all the answers. It's not. Leadership is asking questions and making space for people to answer. That means leadership may not be as glamorous as we thought.

6. **You really have to care.** Most people have a purpose far removed from progress on these things that concern us the most — these deep, daunting, adaptive challenges. A worker might notice issues in accounting are holding the company back but fail to say anything about it. Trying to help fix that accounting situation isn't her top priority.

With thousands of books and workshops on the topic of leadership, you would think it wouldn't be such a rare thing. But it is.

Organizations, communities, companies, governments and families are starving for more leadership; we need more people able to mobilize others to make progress on daunting, adaptive challenges.

To that end:

1. Leadership is an activity, not a position.

2. Anyone can lead, anytime, anywhere.

3. It starts with you and must engage others.

4. Your purpose must be clear.

5. It's risky.

Leadership is heart and soul work. You won't exercise leadership unless you care for the common good. As you will explore throughout your experience, the risks of leadership are too great. Only when your heart and soul pull you toward the greater — *common* — good do the risks of leadership seem worth it.

CHAPTER 2

Preparing for the Experience

When Ed was a student athlete, his coaches always attempted to create practices that mimicked competition. He specifically remembers preparation for one grueling cross-country meet in the hilly terrain of Lawrence, Kansas. One hill on the route was almost completely vertical, or so it felt while running up it. Trees lined the path up this hill, and the coach found a similar hill for the team to practice on in preparation for that meet. His objective was to create an environment that so closely resembled the meet itself that the runners would be best prepared for race day.

The same idea applies in football (full-pad scrimmages), boxing (sparring), basketball (scrimmages) and countless other sports. The practices are often harder than the games.

When Julia was an actor in Chicago, management would invite members of the theater community to attend final dress rehearsals. Actors and directors know that performing for an audience of peers is the best way to mimic the circumstances and generate the healthy anxiety required for an awesome opening night.

One of our frustrations with leadership development has been the inability of teachers to deploy that same strategy used by athletic coaches and theater directors.

We've had extensive experience in the private, public and nonprofit sectors. One thing we have learned is that progress on issues facing our organizations and communities is difficult. And exercising leadership is challenging, risky, consuming and not always fun.

14

Most leadership development experiences do little to replicate the very difficult environment that is organizational and community life. Instead, most leadership programs are relaxing, comfortable, risk-free and fun-filled.

This idea was on our mind when we started the Kansas Leadership Center. We wanted to create leadership programs that would prepare people for the same intensity they face as they exercise leadership to create stronger organizations.

We care about your learning and have spent years crafting an experience designed not only to get you talking about leadership, but exercising more of it. We believe the mixture of teaching methods described here help make that happen. Not every *For the Common Good* experience is designed the same way, but all will use some or all of these methods and learning structures.

The Three-Legged Stool of Instruction

We use three main teaching methods. Lecture isn't one of them. We believe building leadership capacity in others is an exercise of leadership for our faculty. Just sitting back and lecturing or entertaining participants won't cut it. To propel learning, we use Case-in-Point teaching, the case study method and coaching.

Case-in-Point

Case-in-Point, our primary teaching method, is designed to engage and challenge you, perhaps in ways more intense than other classroom environments you have experienced. This approach helps create an environment conducive to deep learning about your leadership behaviors and potential. The method was pioneered at Harvard University and aims to help participants bolster their capacities to make progress and withstand the stresses of leadership. It does so by having them experience leadership challenges in the "here and now," rather than simply discussing leadership concepts.

Leadership is difficult, and there aren't many low-risk environments where we can experiment with becoming more effective. Basketball players prepare themselves for the intensity of games by replicating the same intensity in practice. Case-in-Point provides its own "practice game" for the exercise of civic leadership. Participants learn and practice competencies necessary for making progress while working within the intensity of a group setting.

In Case-in-Point, you, your group and the facilitator serve as a case study for discussing leadership. The method is based on the idea that the learning group reflects the same leadership issues that affect people generally (hence the name, Case-in-Point). The discussion focuses on such things as how the group works together, the various roles participants are playing and what assumptions are being made about leadership. Through the method, participants will become more skilled at seeing how groups function as systems, an understanding important for addressing challenges within their own organizations or communities.

Case-in-Point can be quite challenging for participants initially. The facilitator will not be lecturing the group, providing the answers or even doing most of the talking. Because participants share the responsibility of leading the discussion with the facilitator, they play an important role in helping direct the group's learning. It is also common for facilitators to ask provocative questions and challenge the interpretations being made by participants. This is done solely for the purpose of helping the group learn by fully exploring its ideas and approaches to leadership.

Most participants ultimately find learning through Case-in-Point to be a rewarding, beneficial experience; however, many do not feel that way at first. It is common to feel confused, frustrated or even upset at times during a program taught using Case-in-Point. Feeling disoriented is a natural part of the learning process as we wrestle with incorporating new ideas into our lives. **In moments when you feel uncomfortable, remain curious and open to new possibilities.**

Here are some other suggestions that may help.

1. **Listen and participate.** Getting the most out of Case-in-Point means talking some of the time and listening some of the time, but never doing either all the time.

2. **Be respectful, purposeful and authentic.** Show consideration for others, but be willing to raise and discuss difficult issues to benefit the group's learning.

3. **Be open to exploring multiple interpretations.** Be willing to ponder explanations you do not agree with and offer educated guesses that may not be "right" or represent your own beliefs. It is OK to say, "One interpretation may be..."

4. **Respect confidentiality.** To allow all participants to be fully candid, it is important not to let the personal data being shared by others leave the room.

5. **Be willing to "play" with it.** Case-in-Point represents an opportunity to stretch yourself by trying out new approaches on the "practice field" rather than the "playing field." It is hard to learn anything from it until one is willing to try something new.

6. **Enjoy the ride.** Despite having differing opinions and backgrounds, participants tend to be united by their aspiration to build stronger organizations and communities. The chance to be in the room and discuss how to make progress on important issues represents a precious opportunity to learn, grow and enjoy.

Case Study

The case study method is utilized in many *For the Common Good* experiences, giving participants the opportunity to analyze challenging leadership situations in a variety of settings. This learning method usually begins with participants reading or viewing a description of a real-life dilemma. Participants are asked to put themselves in the shoes of the case protagonist as they analyze the situation and discuss the best ways forward.

The following tips will help you get the most from our case studies.

1. **Focus on the leadership dilemma.** The point of each case is to learn about leadership. Don't become too preoccupied with the other details and variables. Zero in on the challenges the protagonist is facing related to mobilizing others to make progress on difficult work.

2. **Don't be the expert in the room.** Be reluctant to claim expertise. For example, just because a case is set in a political setting doesn't mean someone with political experience has more expertise on the situation.

3. **Stick to the information in the case.** From time to time a participant may have actual experience with the characters or situation described in a case. Resist the urge to add information or perspectives not contained in the original case material.

4. **Engage with other participants, not just the facilitator.** Speak to your colleagues rather than directly to the facilitator. The goal is a robust discussion among members of the group. State your opinion. Ask questions of your colleagues. Debate the case and discover together.

5. **Offer ideas and interpretations.** A case study session works best if participants are willing to offer lots of ideas and interpretations about the case. Think out loud. Don't wait until you have the perfect contribution. More ideas are better for a case discussion.

Coaching

Research shows coaching speeds and sustains your ability to apply what you learn. It is not enough to attend a workshop or read a book about leadership. To make real change, individuals and teams must put ideas into action, try new approaches and be willing to learn from successes and failures. A coach is a partner in this journey.

Coaching provides enormous value for developing individuals and their organizations. In most of our programs, you'll have a chance to work one-on-one with our leadership coaches to increase your effectiveness. Coaching helps you make better decisions, practice new actions, gain deep insight into yourself and your situation and build confidence.

Frequently Asked Questions about Our Coaching

1. **What is leadership coaching?**
   Coaching is a supportive partnership as you apply the *For the Common Good* learning to make more progress. We offer coaching in multiple formats. For instance, three 30-minute coaching sessions are included in most programs as you apply what you learn.

2. **How much time will it take?**
   Most programs include three 30-minute conversations with your coach. To maximize learning and progress, do your best to complete your coaching within six weeks of your program experience. If you are participating in a program for teams, you may also have access to coaching as a team.

3. **How do I get matched with a coach?**
   You will typically choose your coach from among our diverse team of trained and certified leadership coaches. A staff member will facilitate the matching process. In team programs, your coach may be assigned by KLC staff.

4. **What if I want more coaching?**
   Many people find coaching a valuable form of professional development and support. Talk with our staff about fees and scheduling if you wish to extend your work with your leadership coach past the first three sessions included in the cost of the program.

Making the Most of Coaching

You gain substantial value if you simply put the times on your calendar and show up for each session with your coach. Your coach will help you:

- Make sense of your *For the Common Good* experience. If an idea or activity intrigued, frustrated or confused you, your coach can help you determine how it applies to your life and work.

- Diagnose your situation and experiment with using the *For the Common Good* competencies to make progress on what you care about most.

- Gain insight into the way you manage yourself.

- Enjoy and learn from these conversations focused squarely on you.

Ideas to help get the most out of coaching:

1. **Spend a few minutes preparing for each call or meeting.** Clear your desk. Close your email. Jot down a few notes about what you want to be different as a result of the conversation.

2. **Prioritize coaching in your schedule.** Coaching is part of your long-term commitment to making progress on what you care about. Schedule all of your calls at once. Resist the urge to postpone or cancel for other meetings or tasks. Talk with your boss or team about why it's important to keep your appointment.

3. **Think cumulatively.** The value of coaching at the Kansas Leadership Center is cumulative. Each session builds upon the others to help you make progress and apply what you've learned.

4. **Translate your learning into real life.** Work with your coach to identify relevant pages in this book. Experiment with new ideas between coaching sessions.

5. **Dig below the surface.** Let your coach know what's going on in your heart and your gut. Confide your values. Let your coach know where you find the greatest meaning in life.

6. **Have an end in mind, but also go with the flow.** Some of the best coaching conversations happen when you have a clear idea of what you want to accomplish, but sometimes coaching will catch you by surprise: The conversation shifts and you gain an insight or develop an action plan you could never have imagined.

Different Learning Structures

We're not sure leadership can be taught, but we are confident it can be learned, and we view our job as creating the environment for that learning to take place. To that end, we structure several different types of learning environments for your experience.

Large Group

You'll spent time with all of your fellow participants, whether your program has 10 or 200 people. Case-in-Point is most often utilized in a larger group setting, although not usually with more than 70 or 80. Diversity of opinion in the large group strengthens the experience for everyone and enriches learning. Don't shy away from jumping into the discussion. If that is difficult for you, share your thoughts with a colleague during a break or take advantage of discussion time in small groups to gain confidence.

Small Group

You will likely be assigned to a small group to experience the peer consulting process or our team coaching experience. Both processes are designed to help you learn and apply the leadership ideas. We encourage you to view your small group experience as another environment in which to practice exercising leadership. Viewing it simply as a place to talk about leadership will rob you and others of an incredible learning opportunity.

Partners

In some exercises, you'll be asked to engage in a series of discussions with a fellow participant of the program. We've found listening to and engaging with a partner is particularly helpful for some activities. Partners will be selected informally and "in the moment."

Informal Time

We know learning continues outside the classroom. Meals, breaks and social times are a great opportunity to engage your fellow participants to discuss ideas you find challenging or inspiring.

Online

We are integrating more and more online material into our in-person experiences to help you refine your thinking about the ideas. A member of our team will contact you about online pre-program work.

Individual Reflection

You'll be encouraged to take time during the program, and on your own, to reflect in writing using this workbook or your own journal. Use your reflection time to think deeply, brainstorm, draw connections to your own life, make practical meaning of the lessons you are learning and jot down questions to discuss with peers and teachers.

CHAPTER 3

Four Competencies of Leadership

The original version of this chapter appeared as an article in the first issue of our magazine, *The Journal*. It's been a standard reading for participants in our programs ever since. While civic in orientation, this article provides a foundation for ideas useful to all participants regardless of civic or private sector.

The Four Competencies offer a framework, born out of listening to Kansans, for effective leadership. Think about any failed effort at making change happen, and chances are one or more of the Four Competencies was absent. Conversely, successful leadership efforts tend to embody these simple, yet profound competencies. The Four Competencies represent the type of leadership needed to truly create stronger organizations and communities.

Most everyone intimately involved with the Kansas Leadership Center (board, staff, faculty and advisors) has significant experience in public, nonprofit and/or private life. We mention this not to pat ourselves on the back (there is a difference between being involved and being effective, after all — more on that later), but as a way of conveying our empathy with those active in trying to build stronger, healthier organizations and communities. Our experience tells us exercising leadership is hard. If it were easy, everyone would be doing it!

We also believe developing leadership capacity in others — which is our charge — is a deep and daunting task that requires more know-how than we collectively possessed when we began this effort in 2007. This led us to design and implement a process of engagement with Kansans about the nature of our state's challenges and the type of leadership necessary to make progress on those challenges.

Our experience, as well as the feedback from listening to Kansans, tells us there is something different about leadership in civic life versus business or organizational life. Of course, there are many similarities, with the main one being that leadership is never easy — anywhere. But we believe leadership is even more difficult in civic life, primarily because no one is in charge. Think about it: In civic life, even the governor has considerably less formal authority than the CEO of any company. To do anything significant, the governor must collaborate with at least the majority of the legislature. It's no easy task to get a majority of people to do anything significant, but at least a CEO can hire, fire, promote, demote, give a bonus or raise, etc.

Leadership is especially difficult in the civic sphere, and if we are going to make progress on creating healthier communities, KLC must help prepare people to exercise a different type of leadership that is especially in touch with civic life.

Rather than just sit around and wax philosophic about what type of leadership is necessary, we instead engaged over 100 Kansans to help us answer the question. All were asked the same questions, and their answers were recorded, transcribed and analyzed. As we explored their answers, four broad leadership competencies emerged. This chapter provides an introduction to those competencies, which have become known simply as the Four Competencies. Our assertion is that significantly greater progress would be made if more people working for the common good — of their community, business, church, etc. — were competent in these areas: diagnose situation, manage self, intervene skillfully and energize others.

Diagnose Situation

What does it mean to diagnose situations for the purpose of exercising effective leadership on difficult challenges? And why is it the first of Four Competencies?

If you are trying to intervene to help make progress on a tough issue, understanding what you are intervening into is critical. Our experience and observation is that the biggest single mistake people make in trying to exercise leadership is in misdiagnosing the situation. Chuck Krider, a longtime godfather of Kansas economic policy, put it this way:

"Problem identification is key. If you don't identify the right problems, then you are working on the wrong thing! What are you going to work on? What are you going to do? To set good objectives and goals, you have to understand the problem."

Why do people misdiagnose the situation? Two reasons stand out.

1. **Don't just stand there; do something.** When a community or organization is facing a difficult issue, there is almost always tremendous pressure, especially on those in authority, to act, to do something, making it difficult to spend the time necessary to do a deep diagnosis. In the complex economic meltdown in the fall of 2008, President George W. Bush and the Congress took unprecedented steps in a matter of days. The public would not have easily tolerated inaction.

2. **Find a pain-free fix, please.** The actions preferred by others are those that address the manifestations of the crisis with as little cost or pain as possible. The hurry-up legislation enacted to deal with the economic crisis was designed to stem the hemorrhaging rather than address the underlying causes, an approach that illustrates the single biggest diagnostic error people make in framing issues: treating adaptive challenges as if they were technical problems.

Adaptive Challenges

What is an adaptive challenge? And how is it different from a technical problem? Here's a simple example. If the brakes on your car are failing, there is an easy fix: Take the car to a repair shop and hire an expert, a mechanic, who has skills and knowledge that are probably beyond your competence. For you, the problem is beyond your capacity. For the mechanic, it is right in the wheelhouse and can be tackled with a high degree of certainty that the intervention will be successful. But let's say that your 85-year-old father has recently moved in with you. He has been driving your car and, given his failing eyesight, prefers to keep his foot on the brake all the time just in case he needs to stop quickly. Getting new brakes will provide only a temporary fix.

Like most complex problems, your brake problem has elements that are technical — the brakes do not function properly — and aspects that are adaptive — your father has been driving a car for over 60 years and for him driving symbolizes his continuing to lead an independent life, an important part of his self-identity. For him to stop driving would rip part of his heart out.

Technical problems live in people's heads and logic systems. They are susceptible to facts and authoritative expertise. Adaptive challenges live in people's hearts and stomachs. They are about values, loyalties and beliefs. Progress on them requires the people with the problem to do the work, and the work involves refashioning those deeply held beliefs.

You can see why there is always pressure in a community or organization in which you are working to interpret challenges as technical problems.

Here is a Kansas example. Several years ago, the legislature, feeling increased pressure from businesses and individuals, felt it had to act on health care reform. The only problem was we avoided the deep, daunting adaptive challenges related to health care reform — cost, cuts to other state programs, responsibility for government vs. individuals, etc. — and instead went for the technical fix and established what is now known as the Kansas Health Policy Authority (KHPA).

And what happened? For a while, the pressure in the system waned. Legislators could point out that they established the KHPA and had asked the KHPA to develop recommendations for reform. Low and behold, a few years later the KHPA, as requested, delivered a set of health care reform measures to the legislature. The problem was, those recommendations represented many of the same conflictual value choices legislators tried so hard to avoid a few years earlier. What do they value more: health reform or a pledge not to raise taxes? Clean indoor air or the rights of local business owners? More Kansans covered by Medicaid or reducing the size of government?

KHPA is a fine agency, staffed by talented and competent Kansans, and its mission goes beyond simply providing recommendations to the legislature. However, when it comes to health reform, KHPA must wrestle with the reality that its establishment may have been the legislature's attempt at solving an adaptive challenge with a technical solution.

Interpretation of the current reality is an essential first step in exercising leadership so you can tailor your intervention to the situation. In our brake example, your intervention would be very different if you understood that the problem was about undermining your father's sense of independence rather than getting new brakes. Similarly, the U.S. government's intervention into the economic crisis might have

COMMON GOOD

LEADERSHIP COMPETENCIES

DIAGNOSE SITUATION
- Explore tough interpretations
- Distinguish technical and adaptive work
- Understand the process challenges
- Test multiple interpretations and points-of-view
- Take the temperature
- Identify who needs to do the work

MANAGE SELF
- Know your strengths, vulnerabilities and triggers
- Know the story others tell about you
- Choose among competing values
- Get used to uncertainty and conflict
- Experiment beyond your comfort zone
- Take care of yourself

ENERGIZE OTHERS
- Engage unusual voices
- Work across factions
- Start where they are
- Speak to loss
- Inspire a collective purpose
- Create a trustworthy process

INTERVENE SKILLFULLY
- Make conscious choices
- Raise the heat
- Give the work back
- Hold to purpose
- Speak from the heart
- Act experimentally

been very different if the problem were diagnosed as having to reverse the country-wide norm of forgoing savings in favor of consumption — spending beyond our means — rather than preventing bank failures.

How do you interpret reality well? How do you diagnose situations effectively? How do you distinguish technical problems from adaptive challenges when they are often enmeshed and when most everyone around you wants you to accept the technical interpretations? Here are four techniques you might find useful.

First, as your organization or community struggles to deal with a difficult issue, it is a leadership act to help **keep open interpretations that are adaptive, systemic and conflictual rather than technical, individual and benign.** Here's an example. Kansas, like many states, has faced severe budget shortfalls. It would be tempting to diagnose those situations as simply having less money than anticipated to meet projected expenses. That interpretation might well lead, as it often does in government budget crises, to across-the-board cuts. But a more uncomfortable and systemic interpretation might be that the problem is less about a revenue shortfall than about our unwillingness in more flush financial times to make hard decisions about priorities and to save enough money to get us through difficult times. That interpretation would lead to a different set of approaches than across-the-board budget cuts.

It is important to push against our default interpretations, which are often deeply ingrained in us. When discussing how business men and women often diagnose civic life, one of the 100 Kansans we interviewed said, "... a lot of business folks have this fifth-grade civics book understanding of how the public sector works. They apply their model of how the universe works to the civic model they learned in fifth grade. It's more complicated than that." Another said, "We need skepticism. One of the things that has been a hindrance here is that if you hear it from the right source, if the superintendent says it, for example, it must be true." You must be able to push against your default thinking and test multiple interpretations.

Second, interpretations are only a guess — ideally, your best guess at the time. That means your best guess might not be right. So when you are engaged with others in trying to name and frame the issue, it is important to **hold on to multiple interpretations** rather than gravitating toward the first one that gains broad acceptance or meets the need to "just do something." Test several interpretations simultaneously. Dr. Bob Moser, a family practice doctor in Tribune, Kansas, and current secretary of the Kansas Department of Health and Environment put the challenge of interpretation in civic life this way:

> *"What we need is what I call the family practice model, because we have to go through so many different specialty rotations in medical school. So, you may see five different ways (or interpretations) to repair a particular wound. As you learn more about it, with time, study and evaluation, you take a little of this one and a little of that one."*

Third, adaptive challenges are **often more about process than content.** The merits of an issue are relevant but not controlling. Think more about how you are going to go about making progress than marshaling the facts and making the best argument for your preferred solution.

Ron Hammerschmidt, a former longtime Kansas Department of Health and Environment employee, suggested people tend to get an "A" in commitment to their cause, but a "D" or "F" in understanding what really needs to be done. What really needs to be done, at least for adaptive challenges, tends to be more about process than content.

Finally, if you are trying to find the underlying deeper, adaptive challenge, look for where there is conflict or pain, where the heat is in the system, where the disequilibrium is high. All of those signal an adaptive issue is at hand.

Diagnosis is an art, not a science. But it is an essential skill in the effective exercise of leadership on difficult challenges where progress has been inconsequential or non-existent.

Manage Self

Exercising leadership effectively requires artfully deploying yourself. Artfully deploying yourself requires knowing yourself well enough to make conscious choices about whether you are well situated to intervene and, if so, how to intervene to maximize the chances of success.

What Do You Need to Know About Yourself?

First, with a cool, clear, realistic eye, you need to be able to **identify your own strengths, vulnerabilities and triggers.** Everyone has strengths and weaknesses. Everyone has hot buttons that others can press to take us out of our game. Everyone's packaging is both a resource and a constraint. If you are a well-spoken male, there might be situations where a more plainspoken female would be more effective. If you have a big unfilled need to be liked, then you may not be well suited to delivering unwelcome news with clarity.

Brian Black, corporate public affairs manager for Spirit Aerosystems in Wichita, said, "You get someone who is super-intelligent, who is just extremely bright, but their bedside manner is terrible, so they are ineffective. I know people with Ph.D.s who never had more than an adjunct faculty position, because they just don't get it."

Regarding triggers, or the "hot buttons" that can set us off, Kay Johnson, director of environmental services for the City of Wichita, said, "We need to have a commitment to not give up, get mad, take our toys and go home!" Understanding what might trigger us to "take our toys and go home" is critical to managing yourself for the difficult task of civic leadership.

Second, and closely related to the first, you **need to know the story others tell about you.** How are you understood? What is your formal authority? What is your informal authority? Are you considered an expert on certain issues? What is your reputation? What is the folklore about your past performance and involvement? If you are new to the community, you have certain advantages and certain disadvantages. If you supported the winning candidate for mayor, you are in a different place than if you supported her unsuccessful challenger. If you are a businessperson, then your stepping out on an issue that is seen to be pro-business will be less effective than if you are a prominent environmentalist.

Third, you need to **distinguish yourself from your role.** When you are contemplating intervening to help make progress on a challenge that has been persistent in spite of previous attempts, people will come at you personally, with both praise and pushback. But you are neither saint nor sinner: It is not about you. Your initiative is a role you are playing at a moment in time, helping your community or organization address a tough problem, and that activity will generate all sorts of emotions, which may well be directed at you. Taking them personally, thinking they are about you and not about the role you are playing, will be a diversion. On this note, prominent Kansas historian Craig Miner said:

> *"I have been very impressed by some politicians' patience. Sometimes I'm not impressed by much else about them. Sometimes they are listening to things that are quite abusive and not losing their cool or demeanor or feeling that people do have a right to express their opinions."*

Since you are likely to be part of any system you are trying to change, a member of the community or organization you are trying to move from the current reality to an aspired future, you are part of the problem and will need to change as well. This suggests two other elements of managing yourself.

Fourth, **identify and choose among your own competing values.** What has held you back from intervening in the past, and what risks have you not been willing to take? If you can figure out what your own competing values are, such as being liked versus being respected, then you can also begin to assess whether you are willing to take the loss potentially associated with choosing among them. Embedded within this fourth concept is the ability to have the courage to accept risk and tolerate dissent while elevating a value for the common good over your own advancement.

Exercising leadership often requires us to put at risk our personal stakes for the common good. Leadership is risky business and requires tremendous courage.

Mary Birch, one of Ed's longtime mentors and the former president of the Overland Park Chamber of Commerce, said, "Leadership requires head, heart, guts and courage. And courage is the one I find missing the most."

A core value for everyone, according to Joe Harkins, longtime civil servant and leadership scholar at the University of Kansas, is doing what feels right. He said:

> *"Every human being, according to Sigmund Freud, is hard-wired to seek pleasurable experiences and avoid unpleasant ones. ... But that very instinctive drive in human beings is the Achilles heel for leadership. So you have to find people who have the ability to recognize the instinctive response when they experience it and override it. Leadership requires acting in unnatural ways. You have to willingly, consciously take on unpleasant tasks because they probably got to be a problem because everyone else was avoiding them. And that requires an extraordinary degree of self-awareness."*

Fifth, beware of the tendency to make a moral principle out of being reluctant to do something that is really uncomfortable for you to do. It is important to do what is needed, not what is comfortable.

For example, most people do not like to ask difficult questions of their friends, colleagues, peers or authority figures. But sometimes, forcing people to deal with difficult questions is exactly what is necessary to make progress. If you refuse to ask difficult questions, it may be tempting to say, "It's not right to put people on the defensive that way," rather than, "I know that is the right thing to do here, but it just makes me feel bad." Exercising leadership on tough challenges will undoubtedly require you to get outside of your own preferred behavior, your own comfort zone. You will have to do what is needed, not what is comfortable.

Again, Harkins' words are illustrative:

"All of us have an incredible ability to rationalize our behavior. We can sidestep and avoid unpleasant situations with grace and dignity and convince ourselves that it's the right thing to do. We're deceiving ourselves and avoiding leadership. We talk ourselves into avoiding it and go on with our business. So the ability to recognize and override the pleasure principle is a fundamental leadership characteristic."

To manage yourself well requires a lot of self-awareness, not only of who you are as a human being, but also of who you are in the particular situation into which you are planning to intervene. In a sense, you are being asked to understand yourself deeply both in human terms and in political terms. This is no easy task. Often your view of yourself on either dimension is different than how you are perceived. For that reason, it is useful to reality-check your own assessment with trusted others who can help keep you from making a misstep based on some assumptions that are part of your own self-identity but do not match how you are experienced by others.

Finally, you can't manage self, let alone exercise leadership, without **taking care of yourself.** Although the results are worth it, exercising leadership will wear you down. Making progress on adaptive challenges can't be done overnight and therefore requires you and others to stay engaged for the long haul. Burnout is not a leadership behavior. Take care of yourself — physically, emotionally, spiritually, socially, etc. — and you'll be able to exercise leadership more effectively.

Intervene Skillfully

If you keep doing what you have always been doing, nothing is going to change. Leadership is about change. The catalyst for change is often an intentional, well-designed intervention. Intervening skillfully is the third of Four Competencies.

Individuals and organizations "intervene" into organizations and communities to attempt progress on things they care about. A church notices an increasing number of homeless families and intervenes by opening a shelter and providing job training. At a neighborhood homeowners association meeting, an individual realizes the meetings constantly revolve around technical issues such as dues and trash pickup and intervenes to focus part of the conversation on how the neighborhood can begin building neighborly bonds among residents. A middle manager discovers unproductive tension between marketing and sales and intervenes to build bridges between those factions.

It is important to think of interventions, or leadership in general, as able to come from anywhere, not just the positional authority figures. In fact, communities and organizations will be better off as soon as we quit thinking about leadership as positional and start thinking of it as an activity.

Doing this allows us to analyze what behaviors and attributes make up the visible activity of leadership. We often refer to the "visible activity of leadership" as interventions.

Mayors, city council members, county commissioners, state legislators, nonprofit executives and business CEOs are often referred to as "leaders." Why? Because they have an authority title, and in most places in life, authority and leadership are synonymous. The authority figures in the state legislature — speaker of the house, senate president, etc. — are called legislative leadership. The authority figures in a company — CEO, CFO, COO, etc. — are often called the leadership team. When people complain about the leadership of their city, more often than not, they are referring to the city council members. All of these individuals are authority figures; whether they ever exercise leadership is a completely different question.

Are they experimenting in hopes of making real progress on the community's most daunting challenges? Are their interventions leading to real change? Simply holding the authority role is not enough.

Eric Sexton, longtime government relations director for Wichita State University and current WSU athletic director, put it this way:

"Being able to stand up and make a speech is not leadership. It [leadership] is about how you engage people. I am talking about leadership that moves communities, states and neighborhoods. … Just because someone is not viewed as an [authority figure] doesn't mean they are not driving a system, a process or a decision."

The ability of more people to intervene skillfully in community or organizational life is critical. But understanding the concept of intervening — or of leadership as an activity — is only part of the equation. We need to learn how to intervene skillfully

What makes interventions effective? People who exercise leadership are intentional about when, why and how they intervene into a system or organization. They resist intervening in whatever way feels most natural to them (i.e., their "default"— see Manage Self), **but instead make conscious choices about what type of intervention is needed to fit the situation.** Dale Dennis is the deputy commissioner of education in Kansas. He has been with the Department of Education since the 1960s and has worked closely with the Kansas Legislature all those years. He referred to the idea of conscious choices in describing members of the House of Representatives:

"Some of them went to the microphone and talked all the time. Those that didn't accepted the reality that leadership often includes making choices about when to speak!"

People who excel at intervening skillfully in leadership calculate how best to capture the attention of their desired audience (e.g., protest, steady engagement, etc.). These individuals understand and appreciate the role and necessity of conflict in making progress on daunting issues. Conflict is not seen as something always to be avoided, but rather something that may be a necessary part of the process. They have diagnosed the situation well enough to know whether their intervention should be designed to increase or decrease conflict.

Intervening skillfully also means resisting the temptation to put all the work on their shoulders. Giving the work of identifying the challenges and possible solutions back to the usual and unusual factions involved with the challenge engages stakeholders in powerful ways. This is different than delegating, which usually involves telling someone else exactly what you want him or her to do. This is the riskiest of the competencies. Once you begin an intervention, you lose control of the outcome. Diagnosing the situation and managing self, the first two competencies, are critical but not inherently risk-laden.

At the heart of this competency are two beliefs. First, leadership is about activity (interventions), not position (authority); second, effective interventions are intentionally designed and delivered.

At its core, leadership on daunting challenges is about emotions more than cold, hard facts.

A few years ago, the Kansas Legislature was debating a bill to require young children to sit on a booster seat in automobiles. In the eyes of advocates, the cold, hard facts suggested the law should be passed; in fact, several studies suggested implementation of the law would immediately begin to save lives in Kansas.

To the disbelief of these advocates, the bill had lingered for years. Finally, in 2006 a state legislator who had a young family, including a child with special physical needs, went to the well of the House to speak passionately on behalf of the bill. His speech contained no facts. Instead, he spoke with first-hand knowledge of raising a child with special needs. As he **spoke from his heart,** the bill's passage became more likely. Toward the end of his speech, he implored, "It will be worth it if this bill helps just one child not face what my daughter has faced." No facts. No figures. The bill passed later that day.

Through the years, dozens of legislators had spoken at the well in support of the bill. Many were fine orators, but none spoke from the depth of such great personal experience as this legislator. By speaking from his heart, he created the space for others to do the same through their words and votes.

At the heart of intervening skillfully is the belief you can't change people's values; they have to change them. Intervening skillfully is about creating the conditions for people to begin changing their values in a lasting way.

Energize Others

The fourth competency is energizing others. Leadership is not a solitary activity. The best idea or intervention goes nowhere without others taking up the cause. For example, someone passionate about helping low-income Kansans build assets doesn't get very far if he can't embolden dozens of additional champions for the cause. No one individual or entity can tackle a daunting challenge alone. Leadership on these challenges must involve energizing more people to take up the difficult work of leadership.

Central to energizing others is figuring out where they are coming from. What do they care about and what do they need? People tend to get energized when they perceive you care about their situation and their issues. The adage "it is better to be interested than interesting" applies here. To be effective at energizing others, you need to **start where they are, not where you are.**

The temptation, of course, is to have a firm understanding of where other like-minded people are coming from, but to make little effort at understanding where our opponents are coming from. Quite frankly, it is easier to vilify them than to seek to understand them. But making progress on adaptive challenges more often than not requires you to engage with numerous factions. One faction alone simply can't make enough progress.

Discovering "where they are" can best be done by intense engagement. The purpose of the engagement is not to sell them on your idea, but to empower them to help design the intervention. You have to be open to (and want) new possibilities that go beyond or in a different direction than your initial preferred solution. Don't defend your idea, but let the group work on it and make it better or throw it out.

People effective at exercising leadership also intervene in a manner that engages **people across factions in a collaborative and inclusive way.** Their activity in groups tends to bring disparate individuals together to address daunting issues facing the broader community or organization. One of the Kansans we interviewed in developing the Four Competencies described a barrier to leadership not being a lack of willingness to engage across factions, but a lack of knowing how to do it. He said, "It's the ability to go from their own universe to the next."

Especially important to leadership in community life, these individuals purposefully seek ways to **engage an expansive and unusual group of citizens,** rather than relying on the same iconic, or exclusive, depending on your perspective, small group of individuals to develop and implement solutions. For example, rather than relying on the "city officials" to devise a plan for the revitalization of downtown, an individual skilled in civic leadership would instead engage the "city officials" and numerous other individuals or factions that have a stake in downtown revitalization. A skilled leader realizes that diverse minds, reflective of the many factions in the broader community, devise stronger and more sustainable solutions than any one or two factions could on their own. Another interviewee said, "For progress, there need to be other ideas that come into the mix."

In addition, people are energized when they see or can envision progress on their purpose. More importantly, discovering a collective purpose and consistently **orienting to that purpose** is critical to energizing others. It creates hope within organizations and communities. High-performing communities are high-hope communities. Orienting to purpose reminds coalitions, factions and individuals why they are engaged in the difficult work of leadership.

On one hand, energizing others is about empowerment, engagement and collective purpose — all of which tend to have a positive orientation. On the other hand, overcoming difficult challenges will require significant change, and change usually means loss, or at least perceived loss for some. Rather than sugarcoat the bad news or pretend it does not exist, it is actually energizing for others to hear someone **speak to their loss.** The losses need to be acknowledged, not suppressed.

Because real or perceived loss is involved with any significant change effort, you must pace the work of the group or community. People need to be ripe for change. Nothing zaps the energy out of people faster than forcing too much change on them too quickly. Conversely, not asking enough out of people who are ready and willing is also a recipe for failure to energize others.

The Four Competencies offer an easy-to-remember yet difficult-to-execute framework for leadership. Our companies and communities will be better off with more people exercising these ideas more often.

CHAPTER FOUR

Adaptive Work

By Ronald A. Heifetz

(Publisher's note: This article is typically distributed to *For the Common Good* participants prior to their program experience. We encourage you to read it before the first day of your program. The KLC Press purchased the rights to reprint the article here.)

RONALD A. HEIFETZ is co-founder of the Center for Public Leadership at the Kennedy School of Government. This essay is adapted from an entry in the Encyclopedia of Leadership, Sage Publications, 2004.

Our language fails us in many aspects of our lives, entrapping us in a set of cultural assumptions like cattle herded by fences into a corral. Gender pronouns, for example, corral us into teaching children that God is a he, distancing girls and women from the experience of the divine in themselves.

Our language fails us, too, when we discuss, analyze and practice leadership. We commonly talk about leaders in organizations or politics when we actually mean people in positions of managerial or political authority. Although we have confounded leadership with authority in nearly every journalistic and scholarly article written on leadership during the last 100 years, we know intuitively that these two phenomena are distinct when we complain all too frequently in politics and business that "the leadership isn't exercising any leadership," by which we actually mean to say that "people in authority aren't exercising any leadership."

Whether people with formal, charismatic or otherwise informal authority actually practice leadership on any given issue at any moment in time ought to remain a separate question answered with wholly different criteria from those used to define a relationship of formal or informal authority.

As we know, all too many people are skilled at gaining authority, and thus a following, but do not then lead.

Moreover, we assume a logical connection between the words "leader" and "follower," as if this dyad were an absolute and inherently logical structure. It is not. The most interesting leadership operates without anyone experiencing anything remotely similar to the experience of "following." Indeed, most leadership mobilizes those who are opposed or who sit on the fence, in addition to allies and friends. Allies and friends come relatively cheap; it's the people in opposition who have the most to lose in any significant process of change.

When mobilized, allies and friends become not followers but active participants — employees or citizens who themselves often lead in turn by taking responsibility for tackling tough challenges, often beyond expectations and often beyond their authority. They become partners. And when mobilized, opposition and fence-sitters become engaged with the issues, provoked to work through the problems of loss, loyalty and competence embedded in the change they are challenged to make. Indeed, they may continue to fight, providing an ongoing source of diverse views necessary for the adaptive success of the business or community. Far from becoming "aligned" and far from any experience of "following," they are mobilized by leadership to wrestle with new complexities that demand tough trade-offs in their ways of working or living. Of course, in time they may begin to trust, admire and appreciate the person or group that is leading, and thereby confer informal authority on them, but they would not generally experience the emergence of that appreciation or trust by the phrase, "I've become a follower."

This puts the struggle to reform public services to produce radically better social outcomes for citizens in an important new light. It may mean that policies for "leadership" must go beyond conferring extra authority or heaping greater expectation on those who occupy positions of public authority. It places a premium instead on mobilizing a more responsible citizenship, which includes the "embracing" of people actively opposed to the direction and manifestations of change. Perhaps most important, it means that public deliberation and public debate about the normative value of the goals toward which leadership energy is directed take on crucial importance.

If leadership is different from the capacity to gain formal or informal authority, and therefore different from the ability to gain a "following" attracting influence and accruing power, what can anchor our understanding of it?

Leadership takes place in the context of problems and challenges. Indeed, it makes little sense to describe leadership when everything and everyone in an organization is humming along just fine, even when processes of influence and authority will be virtually ubiquitous in coordinating routine activity. Leadership becomes necessary to businesses and communities when people have to change their ways rather than continue to operate according to current structures, procedures and processes. Beyond technical problems, for which authoritative and managerial expertise will suffice, adaptive challenges demand leadership that can engage people in facing challenging realities and then changing at least some of their priorities, attitudes and behavior in order to thrive in a changing world.

Mobilizing people to meet adaptive challenges, then, is at the heart of leadership practice. In the short term, leadership is an activity that mobilizes people to meet an immediate challenge. In the medium and long term, leadership generates new cultural norms that enable people to meet an ongoing stream of adaptive challenges in a world that will likely pose an ongoing set of adaptive realities and pressures. Thus, with a longer view, leadership develops an organization or community's adaptive capacity or adaptability. This investment in adaptability should be part of the social vision offered by political leadership, as well as part of the organizational strategies that constitute the reform process. In this short article, we suggest seven different ways to describe and understand adaptive work.

The Adaptive Challenge

First, an adaptive challenge is a problem situation for which solutions lie outside the current way of operating. We can distinguish technical problems, which are amenable to current expertise, from adaptive challenges, which are not. Although every problem can be understood as a gap between aspirations and reality, technical problems present a gap between aspirations and reality that can be closed through applying existing know-how. For example, a patient comes to his doctor with an infection, and the doctor uses her knowledge to diagnose the illness and prescribe a cure.

In contrast, an adaptive challenge is created by a gap between a desired state and reality that cannot be closed using existing approaches alone. Progress in the situation requires more than the application of current expertise, authoritative decision-making, standard operating procedures or culturally informed behaviors. For example, a patient with heart disease may need to change his way of life: diet, exercise, smoking and the imbalances that cause unhealthy stress. To make those changes, the patient will have to take responsibility for his health and learn his way to a new set of priorities and habits. This distinction is summarized in Figure 1. (Page 44)

The Demand for Learning

Second, adaptive challenges demand learning. An adaptive challenge exists when the people themselves are the problem and when progress requires a retooling, in a sense, of their own ways of thinking and operating. The gap between aspirations and reality closes when they learn new ways. Thus, a consulting firm may offer a brilliant diagnostic analysis and set of recommendations, but nothing will be solved until that analysis and those recommendations are lived in the new way that people operate. Until then, the consultant has no solutions, only proposals.

Figure 1.

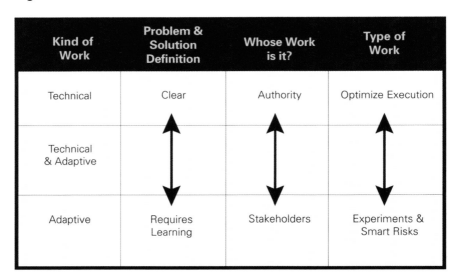

Kind of Work	Problem & Solution Definition	Whose Work is it?	Type of Work
Technical	Clear	Authority	Optimize Execution
Technical & Adaptive	↕	↕	↕
Adaptive	Requires Learning	Stakeholders	Experiments & Smart Risks

Courtesy of Cambridge Leadership Associates

Shift Responsibility to the Stakeholders

Third, adaptive challenges require a shift in responsibility from the shoulders of the authority figures and the authority structure to the stakeholders themselves. In contrast to expert problem-solving, adaptive work requires a different form of deliberation and a different way of taking responsibility. In doing adaptive work, responsibility needs to be felt in a far more widespread fashion. At best, an organization would have its members know that there are many technical problems for which looking to authority for answers is appropriate and efficient, but that for the adaptive set of challenges looking to authority for answers becomes self-defeating.

When people make the classic error of treating adaptive challenges as if they were technical, they wait for the person in authority to know what to do. He or she then makes a best guess, probably just a guess, while the many sit back and wait to see whether the guess pans out. And frequently enough, when it does not, people get rid of that executive and go find another one, all the while operating under the illusion that "if only we had the right 'leader,' our problems would be solved." Progress is impeded by inappropriate dependency, and thus a major task of leadership is the development of responsibility-taking by stakeholders themselves.

Distinguish Between the Essential and the Expendable

Fourth, an adaptive challenge requires people to distinguish between what is precious and essential and what is expendable within their culture. In cultural adaptation, the job is to take the best from history, leave behind that which is no longer serviceable, and through innovation learn ways to thrive in the new environment.

Therefore, adaptive work is inherently conservative as well as progressive. The point of innovation is to conserve what is best from history as the community moves into the future. As in biology, a successful adaptation takes the best from its past set of competencies and loses the DNA that is no longer useful. Thus, unlike many current conceptions of culturally "transforming" processes, many of which are ahistorical — as if one begins all anew — adaptive work, profound as it may be in terms of change, must honor ancestry and history at the same time that it challenges them.

Adaptive work generates resistance in people because adaptation requires us to let go of certain elements of our past ways of working or living, which means to experience loss: loss of competence, loss of reporting relationships, loss of jobs, loss of traditions or loss of loyalty to the people who taught us the lessons of our heritage. Thus, an adaptive challenge generates a situation that forces us to make tough trade-offs. The source of resistance that people have to change is not resistance to change *per se;* it is resistance to loss. People love change when they know it is beneficial. Nobody gives the lottery ticket back when they win. Leadership must contend, then, with the various forms of feared and real losses that accompany adaptive work.

Anchored to the tasks of mobilizing people to thrive in new and challenging contexts, leadership is not simply about change; more profoundly, leadership is about identifying that which is worth conserving. It is the conserving of the precious dimensions of our past that make the pains of change worth sustaining.

Experimentation

Fifth, adaptive work demands experimentation. In biology, the adaptability of a species depends on the multiplicity of experiments that are being run constantly within its gene pool, increasing the odds that in that distributed intelligence, some diverse members of the species will have the means to succeed in a new context. Similarly, in cultural adaptation, an organization or community needs to be running multiple experiments and learning quickly from these experiments in order to see "which horses to ride into the future."

Appropriate and efficient problem-solving depends on authoritative experts for knowledge and decisive action. In contrast, dealing with adaptive challenges requires a comfort with not knowing where to go or how to move next.

In mobilizing adaptive work from an authority position, leadership takes the form of protecting elements of deviance and creativity in the organization in spite of the inefficiencies associated with those elements. If creative or outspoken people generate conflict, then so be it. Conflict becomes an engine of innovation, rather than solely a source of dangerous inefficiency. Managing the dynamic tension between creativity and efficiency becomes an ongoing part of leadership practice for which there exists no equilibrium point at which this tension disappears. Leadership becomes an improvisation, however frustrating it may be not to know the answers.

The Time Frame of Adaptive Work

Sixth, the time frame of adaptive work is markedly different from that of technical work. It takes time for people to learn new ways to sift through what is precious from what is expendable, and to innovate in ways that enable people to carry forward into the future that which they continue to hold precious from the past. Moses took 40 years to bring the children of Israel to the Promised Land, not because it was such a long walk from Egypt, but because it took that much time for the people to leave behind the dependent mentality of slavery and generate the capacity for self-government guided by faith in something ineffable. Figure 2 depicts this difference in time frame.

Figure 2.

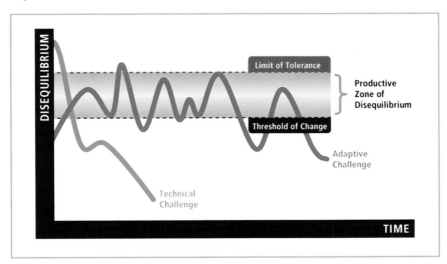

Courtesy of Cambridge Leadership Associates

Because it is so difficult for people to sustain prolonged periods of disturbance and uncertainty, human beings naturally engage in a variety of efforts to restore equilibrium as quickly as possible, even if it means avoiding adaptive work and begging off the tough issues. Most forms of adaptive failure are a product of our difficulty in containing prolonged periods of experimentation, and the difficult conversations that accompany them.

Work avoidance is simply the natural effort to restore a more familiar order, to restore equilibrium. Although many different forms of work avoidance operate across cultures and peoples, it appears that there are two common pathways: the displacement of responsibility and the diversion of attention. Both pathways work terribly well in the short term, even if they leave people more exposed and vulnerable in the medium and long term. Some common forms of displacing responsibility include scapegoating, blaming the persistence of problems on authority, externalizing the enemy or killing the messenger. Diverting attention can take the form of fake remedies, like the Golden Calf; an effort to define problems to fit one's competence; repeated structural adjustments; the faulty use of consultants, committees and task forces; sterile conflicts and proxy fights ("let's watch the gladiator fight!"); or outright denial.

Adaptive Work Is a Normative Concept

Finally, adaptive work is a normative concept. The concept of adaptation arises from scientific efforts to understand biological evolution. Applied to the change of cultures and societies, the concept becomes a useful, if inexact, metaphor. For example, species evolve whereas cultures learn. Evolution is generally understood by scientists as a matter of chance, whereas societies will often consciously deliberate, plan and intentionally experiment. Close to our normative concern, biological evolution conforms to laws of survival. Societies, on the other hand, generate purposes beyond survival. The concept of adaptation applied to culture raises the question: adapt to what, for what purpose?

In biology, the "objective function" of adaptive work is straightforward: to thrive in new environments. Survival of the self and of one's gene-carrying kin defines the direction in which animals adapt.

A situation becomes an adaptive challenge because it threatens the capacity of a species to pass on its genetic heritage. Thus, when a species multiplies its own kind and succeeds in passing on its genes, it is said to be "thriving" in its environment.

Thriving is more than coping. There is nothing trivial in biology about adaptation. Some adaptive leaps transform the capacity of a species by sparking an ongoing and profound process of adaptive change that leads to a vastly expanded range of living.

In human societies, "thriving" takes on a host of values not restricted to survival of one's own kind. At times, human beings will even trade off their own survival for values like liberty, justice and faith. Thus, adaptive work in cultures involves the clarification of values and the assessment of realities that challenge the realization of those values.

Because most organizations and communities honor a mix of values, the competition within this mix largely explains why adaptive work so often involves conflict. People with competing values engage one another as they confront a shared situation from their own points of view. At its extreme, and in the absence of better methods of social change, the conflict over values can be violent. The American Civil War changed the meaning of union and individual freedom. In 1857, ensuring domestic tranquility meant returning escaped slaves to their owners; in 1957, it meant using federal troops to integrate Central High School in Little Rock.

Some realities threaten not only a set of values beyond survival, but also the very existence of a society if these realities are not discovered and met early on by the value-clarifying and reality-testing functions of that society. In the view of many environmentalists, for example, our focus on the production of wealth rather than on coexistence with nature has led us to neglect fragile factors in our ecosystem. These factors may become relevant to us when finally they begin to challenge our central values of health and survival, but by then we may have paid a high price in damage already done, and the costs of and odds against adaptive adjustment may have increased enormously.

Conclusion

Adaptive work, then, requires us to deliberate on the values by which we seek to thrive, and demands diagnostic inquiry into the realities we face that threaten the realization of those values. Beyond legitimizing a convenient set of assumptions about reality, beyond denying or avoiding the internal contradictions in some of the values we hold precious, and beyond coping, adaptive work involves proactively seeking to clarify aspirations or develop new ones, and then involves the very hard work of innovation, experimentation and cultural change to realize a closer approximation of those aspirations by which we would define "thriving."

This constitutes a challenge for our systems of democracy, as well as those of governance and public service delivery. The forms of thriving that public services should support do not remain static. The ways in which they can or should be supported must be tested by public deliberation and by organizational experimentation. Yet citizens are generally ill-prepared for legislation or policy framed as "experimentation." All too often citizens crave solutions, not trial efforts or pilot projects, and therefore put a great deal of pressure on politicians and public servants to overstate the promise of new policies and programmatic instruments. When those promises then fall short, trust in government erodes further.

Thus a central task of democratic leadership is to educate citizens in the difference between technical and adaptive work so that they are prepared to entrust public officials who tell them the truth rather than pander when no easy answers are readily at hand.

The normative tests of adaptive work, then, involve an appraisal of the processes by which orienting values are clarified in an organization or community, and the quality of reality testing by which a more accurate rather than convenient diagnosis is achieved. By these tests, for example, serving up fake remedies for our collective troubles by scapegoating and externalizing the enemy, as was done in extreme form in Nazi Germany, might generate throngs of misled supporters who readily grant to charlatans extraordinary authority in the short run, but it would not constitute adaptive work. Nor would political efforts to gain influence and authority by pandering to people's longing for easy answers constitute leadership. Indeed, misleading people is likely over time to produce adaptive failure.

CHAPTER FIVE

Naming Your Leadership Challenge

The *For the Common Good* experience will ask you to choose a current situation or challenge you are facing. This is for the purpose of your learning and application, and to help you make progress on something you care about. After all, making progress on things people care deeply about is the mission of leadership.

We will ask you to think about your challenge throughout the program, giving you an opportunity to apply what you are learning directly to what you are working on in your organization or community.

Here is a checklist to help identify a good challenge:

- It matters to you.

- You care enough about the issue/situation that you are willing to change your behavior to make progress.

- It's something you are currently working on or have worked on before.

- You need others for progress.

- It's narrowly defined enough that you can do something specific about it (instead of getting rid of world poverty, focus on reducing it in your community, or instead of doubling the size of your organization, focus on increasing growth by a certain percentage.) Keep it to a level that is complex but manageable.

The simplest way to choose a case is to ask yourself the following question: When I think about the future of my organization / family / neighborhood / company / department / etc. (pick one,) what concerns me the most?

You'll be asked to submit answers to the following questions to add definition to the leadership challenge you'll be working on during your *For the Common Good* experience. If you are participating in one of the team programs, you may get extra direction about choosing a challenge that relates to the issue your team is organized around.

These answers will be provided to your small group as described in Section II of this book. Note: We strive to create an environment where all participants appreciate the confidential nature of this exercise. Your written case will be shared with your peers. You are welcome to change the names of people or organizations in your case if you prefer.

We encourage you to take notes here to prepare for your online submission so you'll have a record of your ideas about your leadership challenge in this book.

1. What is the background of the problem/opportunity/challenge? (major players, key events, critical past decisions, etc.)

2. Why is this important to you?

3. What actions have you taken so far, and what actions do you intend to take in the future?

4. What is the question(s) you would most like addressed about your challenge through your *For the Common Good* experience?

After answering these questions, submit your responses online: *www.kansasleadershipcenter.org/leadershipchallenge.* Someone from our staff will contact you with more information prior to your program.

SECTION II

In the Experience

CHAPTER SIX

Peer Consulting

The peer consulting process is a tremendous opportunity to practice, in a controlled setting, the ideas being explored in your program. It's also a way to get feedback from peers about your leadership challenge (sometimes called your "case.") Developed and pioneered by our friends at Cambridge Leadership Associates, this method has been used to help thousands of people across business, government and nonprofits practice and learn to engage in adaptive work.

You will be in a small group of six or seven for this exercise. Throughout your *For the Common Good* experience, you'll meet with your small group three or four times, each time for no more than 90 minutes. Participants will take turns presenting their leadership challenges. The group will then work to better understand each challenge, uncovering perhaps tough interpretations about what's really going on. This process gets high reviews from participants for its uniqueness and structure, which helps individuals see challenges in important new ways and provides an intimate practice ground.

How This Exercise Mimics the Exercise of Leadership: Tips for Success

Most find this exercise helpful. Here are some tips to help it move beyond helpful to profound. Remember, the exercise has two main purposes. One is to help the case presenter get feedback and new perspectives. The other purpose is for you to practice using the very ideas you are learning in your *For the Common Good* experience.

When You Are the Case Presenter

This exercise replicates the demands placed on anyone seeking to exercise leadership in more profound and provocative ways. Serving as the case presenter can be similar to being the authority on a team. When doing adaptive work, the authority's role is often to call attention to the situation and create the conditions for stakeholders to wrestle with it.

1. **Stating the case.** The ability to craft a description, either verbally or on paper, of a tough situation or case and to do it in a way that colleagues can absorb and use to inform their thinking is quite a skill. Organization and community life is full of people unable to coalesce their thoughts constructively, or unable to present the core facts, unable to give the right information to others who are willing and/or interested in helping them. You'll practice that skill with this exercise.

2. **Fielding questions.** Few are good at answering questions. They drone on too long, don't answer with clarity, fail to answer the actual question, get defensive, project unhelpful motives on the questioner, etc. Answering questions quickly and effectively is a skill, as is holding steady while being questioned so your colleagues can learn what they need to learn so they can help you. You'll practice that skill with this exercise.

3. **Holding steady.** Listening to your peers diagnosing your case, without you chiming in can be hard, painful and frustrating. The exercise requires your silence at this stage. Great breakthroughs can happen, in this exercise and in life, when those with the problem (you, in this case) are able to simply hold steady and listen rather than jump in to defend or explain. It's a skill you'll need to lead others to do adaptive work. You'll practice that skill.

4. **Don't pass judgment.** The amount of energy people expend trying to control how they are perceived by others, explaining or defending their actions is enormous. That energy is then unable to be used to explore tough interpretations, understand their part of the mess, etc. Toward the end of the process, you'll have a chance

to reflect on your experience with your group. The temptation, just like in life, will be to explain or defend your actions. Don't. Use this time simply to hold the tough things others said. Don't rush to judgment. It's a skill to engage with those who have said things that don't feel right to you, that might even put you in a bad light. You'll practice that skill in this exercise.

When You Aren't the Case Presenter

Countless opportunities exist to exercise the type of leadership necessary for adaptive work when you are not the case presenter.

1. **Ask good questions.** Knowing why you are asking questions is important. Are you trying to coach someone with your question, such as, "What are your best three options for dealing with this situation?" Are you trying to grill someone with your question, such as, "What did you know, when did you know it and why didn't you do anything about it?" Or, as is the goal in this exercise, are you trying to gain data with your question? Several examples of data-gathering questions are in the instructions to the exercise. Adaptive work requires you to diagnose the situation, and you can't do that without data.

2. **Get beyond your first good idea.** When doing adaptive work, it helps to be unsatisfied with your first good idea. Generating several interpretations of what's happening and several ways forward sets you up to be able to test, or experiment with, lots of things. Holding true to the time frames for this exercise (i.e., 15 minutes for diagnostic brainstorming) will help you practice this skill. Don't end that part early, just keep generating ideas.

3. **Keep trying to diagnose the situation.** One of the biggest mistakes when exercising leadership is trying to solve a challenge before really understanding it. Most of us do this most of the time. Especially when we are in the situation of consulting someone else's situation, it is tempting to offer solutions early and often. But tough challenges are complex and not easily understood. This

exercise forces you to practice by staying in the diagnosis phase longer, a critical skill for leadership.

4. **Raise uncomfortable issues.** It's a leadership behavior to "raise the heat," which often involves saying things that are hard, but necessary, for others to hear. This exercise lets you practice suggesting things that might be uncomfortable for others to hear or for you to mention. Gaining comfort with such activity is a skill of leadership.

How it Works

Each person in your small group will take a turn being the presenter. Below is a suggested time allocation and process for a 45-minute consultation. The proportions are important, especially allocating at least twice as much time to diagnosis than to any of the other components. This is because we get comfortable and attached to our stories, and we need other people to open up and interpret other versions of reality and possibility.

Your group will need to identify the following roles for each consultation:

- Case Presenter: shares an adaptive challenge.

- Facilitator: strictly manages the time boundaries, keeps the case presenter from controlling the conversation and engages others in the process.

- Note-taker: records notes throughout the consultation process and helps the case presenter debrief after the experience.

The timing and goals for each segment should look like this. (Modified from a handout from Cambridge Leadership Associates, used with permission.)

Case presentation **5 minutes**	***Goal for Case Presenter:*** *To present a leadership challenge* • What is the adaptive challenge? • Who are the major players? What are their conflicting perspectives and interests? • What are your strengths with the major players? • What action have you taken or are thinking about taking in reference to the challenge? • What are your real stakes and interests? • Are there any hidden issues? • What have I learned about my adaptive challenge so far?
Data gathering questions **10 minutes**	***Goal for group:*** *To understand the adaptive challenge and the complexities surrounding it and to gather information to help you conduct diagnostic brainstorming in the next phase.* • Who are the major players? What are their formal relationships? Informal alliances? • Where is the senior authority on the issue? • Who are the unusual voices in this situation, and have you sought them out? • What has the presenter done so far to work on the problem? What has the presenter decided not to do? • Why are you working on this? • What do you care about related to this challenge? • What would success look like to the presenter?
Diagnostic brainstorming **15 minutes** ***NOTE: Case Presenter does not speak!**	***Goal for group:*** *To interpret what is happening, offer alternative interpretations and illuminate new ways to understand the case.* • What are the case presenter's stakes: risk of real or anticipated loss, sense of personal competence, pressure to maintain loyalties? • What issues or values does the presenter represent in the case? Do you see/hear competing values? • What are the underlying or hidden issues? What are the value choices each has to make? • How does the situation look to the other players? What is the story they are telling themselves? • What options are off the table for the presenter and why? • What has the presenter contributed to the problem? What is her/his piece of the mess? • What possible adaptive, conflictual or systemic interpretations has the presenter been understandably unwilling to consider? • What is the level of disequilibrium in the system? • What are the relevant factions in this challenge, and what do they care about, who are they loyal to and what are some of their potential losses? • For real change to happen, who has to do the work on this? Who else? • What would it look like for the presenter to "start where they are"? • What would success look like to the players other than the presenter?

Action Step Brainstorming
 	
5 minutes
 	
*NOTE: Case Presenter does not speak!
	Goal for Group: *To offer possible new initiatives, smart risks and experiments for the case presenter to try to move the challenge forward.*
	
	• What smart experiments could be undertaken? Which KLC leadership competency sub points seem relevant?
	  – Does the presenter need to raise or lower the heat?
	  – How might the presenter need to "manage self" differently?
	  – What would it look like for the presenter to "start where they are"?
	• What are low-risk tests of some of the ideas discussed?
	• What courageous conversations need to take place?
	• What new partnerships or relationship shifts need to happen?
	• What could the presenter watch for or monitor as signs of progress on this adaptive challenge?

Presenter reflections **5 minutes**	**Goal for Case Presenter:** *Not to resolve the case! This time is intended for the presenter to share initial reactions to the process and ask specific questions that he/she is now pondering.* • Comment on what has been heard. The idea is that the presenter will "rent" the ideas, trying them out rather than "buying" them or defending against them. • Identify any action step(s) you may undertake in the next six weeks.
Group debrief **5 minutes**	**Goal for group:** *To "get on the balcony" and reflect on how well the consultation went and how to improve in the future.* • What did the group accomplish and what did it avoid? • What default behaviors did participants observe? • Did we make adaptive, conflictual and systemic interpretations? • Did we identify the adaptive challenge? • What could be done to improve consultations in the future?

Traps for the group to watch out for:

- Lack of clarity on the adaptive challenge. Make sure you establish this before moving ahead.

- Presenter will not be able to remain silent and will dominate the conversation, defending and explaining.

- Group members will jump too quickly to solutions, especially technical solutions.

- Group members will be afraid to tell the presenter difficult news or information that would be helpful.

- Group members will "stomp" on others ideas during the "diagnostic brainstorming" and "action step brainstorming" sections of the consultation.

- Presenter will hide real stakes and anxieties.

- Group members will offer insight from their own experience or expertise, rather than see the problem through the eyes of the presenter and other people in the case.

Case presenters often find themselves spinning a bit from the experience. We usually don't let others talk freely about our challenges. It is a good practice both to take a break shortly after the consultation and to have one person check in with the presenter afterwards.

Honesty, forthrightness, initiative, openness, exploration, freedom of expression, curiosity and ruthless compassion are needed for us — whether in an organization or a peer consulting group — to make more progress. Enjoy the use of this exercise. There is much to learn and practice.

Use the following pages for a peer to take notes for you while your challenge is discussed.

Exploring your leadership challenge: Allow a peer to use these blank pages to take notes during your case consultation.

Exploring your leadership challenge: Allow a peer to use these blank pages to take notes during your case consultation.

Exploring your leadership challenge: Allow a peer to use these blank pages to take notes during your case consultation.

Exploring your leadership challenge: Allow a peer to use these blank pages to take notes during your case consultation.

Exploring your leadership challenge: Allow a peer to use these blank pages to take notes during your case consultation.

CHAPTER SEVEN

Applying the Ideas: Your Leadership Playbook

Think of this section as your leadership playbook. This section will help you understand and craft what the exercise of leadership looks like and "move the ball further downfield" in your challenge.

The subsections contain information related to the four leadership competencies: Diagnose Situation, Manage Self, Energize Others and Intervene Skillfully.

We encourage you to write freely in these pages. It's your chance to apply the ideas of the *For the Common Good* experience to your leadership challenge. Our experience suggests working through your challenge in these pages will position you to make more progress on what you care about most.

Diagnose Situation

A problem well stated is a problem half solved.
– Charles Kettering

Leadership Behaviors

1. Actively listen to diverse points of view.

2. Ask open-ended questions of multiple people.

3. Ask for feedback on my conclusions or thinking.

4. Offer alternative ways to proceed.

5. Help others choose among alternative ways of proceeding.

6. Ask probing questions that help others build understanding of a situation.

7. Show awareness of the emotional state of others.

8. Help others develop empathy for and understanding of each other.

9. Help others test their perception of a problem or issue.

10. Seek a deeper understanding of how people work together.

* You'll learn more about the behaviors listed here when you receive your *For the Common Good* 360 Assessment report.

Questions for Reflection

What's the story others are telling about you?

• What surprises you?

• What confirms what you already believe about yourself?

What are all the interpretations you can make of this data?

- Benign (ones that make me feel comfortable)

- Conflictual (ones that challenge the way I usually see myself)

- Individual (ones that attribute my behavior to "who I am")

- Systemic (ones that attribute my behavior to "roles I play in the system")

Identify Factions and What They Care About

Factions are stakeholder groups or individual major players who are involved in or affected by your issue. To make progress, it is important to consider where others stand on the issue. If you hope to engage and energize others, you must start where they are, anticipate and speak to their potential losses, and find connecting interests.

Create a faction map using the diagram on the next page. Take time to identify what each faction values (why they care about this issue), what interests they may share with you and what losses each faction might experience as you attempt to make progress on your leadership challenge. Then, on a scale from 1 to 10 (with 10 being the highest), rate the degree to which each faction cares about your issue and the degree to which you need that faction to make progress.

When you've completed your faction map, ask yourself: Which two or three factions require my attention most? Would framing my challenge more broadly help engage more people?

Faction Map

FACTION: _____

WHY THEY CARE: _____

CONNECTING INTERESTS: _____

_____

LOSSES: _____

Degree to which they care
about my issue (1 to 10)

Degree to which I need them
to make progress (1 to 10)

FACTION: _____

WHY THEY CARE: _____

CONNECTING INTERESTS: _____

_____

LOSSES: _____

Degree to which they care
about my issue (1 to 10)

Degree to which I need them
to make progress (1 to 10)

FACTION: _____

WHY THEY CARE: _____

CONNECTING INTERESTS: _____

_____

LOSSES: _____

Degree to which they care
about my issue (1 to 10)

Degree to which I need them
to make progress (1 to 10)

YOUR ISSUE

FACTION: _____

WHY THEY CARE: _____

CONNECTING INTERESTS: _____

_____

LOSSES: _____

Degree to which they care
about my issue (1 to 10)

Degree to which I need them
to make progress (1 to 10)

FACTION: _____

WHY THEY CARE: _____

CONNECTING INTERESTS: _____

_____

LOSSES: _____

Degree to which they care
about my issue (1 to 10)

Degree to which I need them
to make progress (1 to 10)

FACTION: _____

WHY THEY CARE: _____

CONNECTING INTERESTS: _____

_____

LOSSES: _____

Degree to which they care
about my issue (1 to 10)

Degree to which I need them
to make progress (1 to 10)

FACTION: _____

WHY THEY CARE: _____

CONNECTING INTERESTS: _____

_____

LOSSES: _____

Degree to which they care
about my issue (1 to 10)

Degree to which I need them
to make progress (1 to 10)

FACTION: _____

WHY THEY CARE: _____

CONNECTING INTERESTS: _____

_____

LOSSES: _____

Degree to which they care
about my issue (1 to 10)

Degree to which I need them
to make progress (1 to 10)

FACTION: _____

WHY THEY CARE: _____

CONNECTING INTERESTS: _____

_____

LOSSES: _____

Degree to which they care
about my issue (1 to 10)

Degree to which I need them
to make progress (1 to 10)

FACTION: _____

WHY THEY CARE: _____

CONNECTING INTERESTS: _____

_____

LOSSES: _____

Degree to which they care
about my issue (1 to 10)

Degree to which I need them
to make progress (1 to 10)

FACTION: _____

WHY THEY CARE: _____

CONNECTING INTERESTS: _____

_____

LOSSES: _____

Degree to which they care
about my issue (1 to 10)

Degree to which I need them
to make progress (1 to 10)

Take the Temperature

Conflict is the beginning of consciousness.
– Mary Esther Harding

If you are trying to find the underlying, adaptive elements of your leadership challenge, look for the conflict. Could it be that someone's values are being threatened? If the heat is high, you are probably looking at an adaptive challenge.

Circle a number below to indicate the current temperature of your leadership challenge.

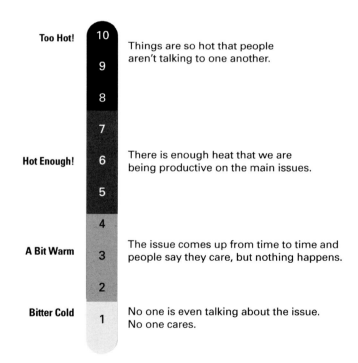

Too Hot!	10	Things are so hot that people aren't talking to one another.
	9	
	8	
	7	
Hot Enough!	6	There is enough heat that we are being productive on the main issues.
	5	
	4	
A Bit Warm	3	The issue comes up from time to time and people say they care, but nothing happens.
	2	
Bitter Cold	1	No one is even talking about the issue. No one cares.

Does the temperature vary among the different factions?

What data or evidence did you use to rate the heat?

Where is the Risk?

Take risks: If it works, much will be accomplished;
if it doesn't, you will be wise.
– Author Unknown

Sometimes the road less traveled is less traveled for a reason.
– Jerry Seinfeld

Leadership is inherently risky. You are trying to change things. People stand to lose, and they won't like it. Be smart. Stay aware of your risks and the risks you are asking others to take.

Mark on the arrow how risky this leadership challenge is for you.

HIGH RISK

LOW RISK

How risky is it for other key players?

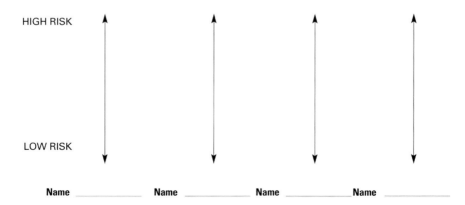

HIGH RISK

LOW RISK

Name _____   Name _____   Name _____   Name _____

Testing Interpretations

The more interpretations we gather, the easier it becomes
to gain a sense of the whole.
– Margaret Wheatley

It's a leadership challenge to hold multiple interpretations of your situation.

Most people jump to technical and benign interpretations. If you wish to lead, explore interpretations that are more adaptive, conflictual and system-oriented. In other words, don't shy away from tough or uncomfortable interpretations.

As you fill out the chart below, ask yourself: Which interpretations are predominant among which factions?

Use this chart to begin thinking about the different types
of work involved in your leadership challenge.

TECHNICAL INTERPRETATIONS What are technical interpretations related to your challenge?	ADAPTIVE INTERPRETATIONS What are adaptive interpretations related to your challenge?
Benign	*Conflictual*
Individual	*Systemic*

Understand the Process Challenges

*It's hard to make a difference when everyone is tangled up
in the rigging of procedural formality and blanketed in fog.*
– Alice Collier Cochran, *Roberta's Rules of Order*

Adaptive challenges are often more about process than content. Think more about how you are going to go about making progress than about making the best argument.

Content challenges include getting and interpreting accurate information, finding policies or model projects that have worked in other communities or hiring the right expert.

Process challenges relate to how you and others work together. Does everyone have the same good information? Are there hidden issues that get in the way of progress? Have the group members had the chance to understand how much they agree or disagree?

Use the chart on the opposite page to identify the process challenges related to your issue. Then rate those challenges on a 1 to 10 scale with 10 being high priority for the success of your leadership challenge and 1 being little or no priority.

Areas you rated highest likely point to where your leadership is needed most.

Rating	Process Challenges

Manage Self

The first and best victory is to conquer self.
– Plato

Leadership Behaviors

1. Remain calm and in control of my emotions.

2. Solicit and respond constructively to feedback from others.

3. Change course based on feedback from others.

4. Keep my ego from getting in the way of progress.

5. Speak believably about openness to others' ideas.

6. Make difficult choices between competing values.

7. Balance personal and professional demands in a healthy way.

8. Seek to understand how others see my position or role in a situation.

9. Maintain energy and commitment in the face of uncertainty, ambiguity and conflict.

10. Seek to identify my strengths and weaknesses.

* You'll learn more about the behaviors listed here when you receive your *For the Common Good* 360 Assessment report.

Questions for Reflection

What are my strengths?

What does the data tell me about my vulnerabilities?

What possible triggers should I be aware of?

What does the feedback say about what I value?

How do I interpret feedback about balancing my personal
and professional demands?

Leverage Your Strengths and Address Your Vulnerabilities

All my life, I always wanted to be somebody.
Now I see that I should have been more specific.
– Jane Wagner

You need to know and manage yourself to lead effectively. Be aware of your default reactions. Know your triggers. Challenge your own assumptions about your strengths and weaknesses. Get to know the story others are telling about you and your issue. Expand your repertoire of possible responses.

Using the diagram on the next page, think about how you see yourself and how others see you in relation to your issue. Use the center section to reflect on how you perceive your role in the situation. Then jot down the names of key factions, considering your strengths and vulnerabilities with each. Think carefully about the story each faction is telling about you and your leadership.

Consider possible experiments to discover more about how you are perceived by people who have a stake in your challenge.

Diagnose Yourself

Faction: _____

My strengths with this faction: _____

Vulnerabilities: _____

Triggers: _____

Story they are telling about me: _____

Faction: _____

My strengths with this faction: _____

Vulnerabilities: _____

Triggers: _____

Story they are telling about me: _____

Faction: _____

My strengths with this faction: _____

Vulnerabilities: _____

Triggers: _____

Story they are telling about me: _____

ME

My current role(s) in the situation:

The role(s) I want to play:

Faction: _____

My strengths with this faction: _____

Vulnerabilities: _____

Triggers: _____

Story they are telling about me: _____

Faction: _____

My strengths with this faction: _____

Vulnerabilities: _____

Triggers: _____

Story they are telling about me: _____

Faction: _____

My strengths with this faction: _____

_____

Vulnerabilities: _____

_____

Triggers: _____

_____

Story they are telling about me: _____

_____

Faction: _____

My strengths with this faction: _____

_____

Vulnerabilities: _____

_____

Triggers: _____

_____

Story they are telling about me: _____

_____

Faction: _____

My strengths with this faction: _____

_____

Vulnerabilities: _____

_____

Triggers: _____

_____

Story they are telling about me: _____

_____

Faction: _____

My strengths with this faction: _____

_____

Vulnerabilities: _____

_____

Triggers: _____

_____

Story they are telling about me: _____

_____

Faction: _____

My strengths with this faction: _____

_____

Vulnerabilities: _____

_____

Triggers: _____

_____

Story they are telling about me: _____

_____

Faction: _____

My strengths with this faction: _____

_____

Vulnerabilities: _____

_____

Triggers: _____

_____

Story they are telling about me: _____

_____

Manage Self

Experiment Beyond Your Comfort Zone

*The self is not something ready-made, but something
in continuous formation through choice of action.*
– John Dewey

*If you believe your good reviews,
you have to believe your bad ones.*
– Anonymous

To make progress on your leadership challenge, you sometimes
have to intervene in ways, or take on roles, that feel uncomfortable
or inconsistent with who you really are. Whatever you do, beware of
criticism or flattery that could divert you from difficult work at hand.
Stay focused on deploying yourself effectively to help the group make
progress.

Complete the table asking yourself: What makes it worth the effort to
work outside of my comfort zone?

List roles or types of interventions necessary to make progress on your challenge. Then rate your level of comfort with each.

ROLE OR INTERVENTION	IN OR OUT OF YOUR COMFORT ZONE?		
	Perfectly comfortable	On the edge	Way outside the zone
	1 2 3 4 5 6 7 8 9 10		
ROLE OR INTERVENTION	IN OR OUT OF YOUR COMFORT ZONE?		
	Perfectly comfortable	On the edge	Way outside the zone
	1 2 3 4 5 6 7 8 9 10		
ROLE OR INTERVENTION	IN OR OUT OF YOUR COMFORT ZONE?		
	Perfectly comfortable	On the edge	Way outside the zone
	1 2 3 4 5 6 7 8 9 10		
ROLE OR INTERVENTION	IN OR OUT OF YOUR COMFORT ZONE?		
	Perfectly comfortable	On the edge	Way outside the zone
	1 2 3 4 5 6 7 8 9 10		
ROLE OR INTERVENTION	IN OR OUT OF YOUR COMFORT ZONE?		
	Perfectly comfortable	On the edge	Way outside the zone
	1 2 3 4 5 6 7 8 9 10		
ROLE OR INTERVENTION	IN OR OUT OF YOUR COMFORT ZONE?		
	Perfectly comfortable	On the edge	Way outside the zone
	1 2 3 4 5 6 7 8 9 10		

Manage Self

Choose Among Your Own Competing Values

Courage is tiny pieces of fear all glued together.
– Terri Guillemets

You are a complex creature. Values and commitments compete for your time and attention every day. Consider, for example, the push and pull between efficiency and inclusiveness, or being liked versus making difficult choices based on current realities. If you want to make progress on your leadership challenge, you must choose among your own competing values.

Complete the table identifying your competing values and evaluating their impact on your ability to manage yourself. Use your insights to help assess risk and mitigate the loss associated with choosing one value over another.

Be honest with yourself here. Don't be afraid to name values that are embarrassing or those easily ignored. Remember, no one needs to see this but you.

How might you begin to work past these competing values to exercise leadership more skillfully?

Value 1	Value 2	Describe the impact of these competing values on your thinking and behavior.

Take Care of Yourself

It's not the load that breaks you down;
it's the way you carry it.
– Lena Horne

As you engage others in difficult work, pay attention to maintaining your own energy and enthusiasm. Take time to renew yourself. Call on friends and colleagues for support. Be purposeful about taking care of yourself for the long haul.

How do you know when your energy is waning?

What activities, practices and places revitalize you?

Whom can you call on for support when you need it?

How might you create time or space to take care of yourself?

Energize Others

There are two ways of spreading light:
to be the candle or the mirror that reflects it.
– Edith Wharton

Leadership Behaviors

1. Instill confidence in others that progress can be made.

2. Help others stay focused on a broader purpose or vision.

3. Engage others in all aspects of an issue, including decisions about how the group will work together and how the issue will be dealt with.

4. Treat others with dignity and respect, regardless of differences.

5. Create opportunities to celebrate small successes that mark progress.

6. Create processes that support and sustain working together.

7. Help others change course when necessary.

8. Engage diverse voices in problem-solving and decision-making.

9. Speak from the heart about what's really important.

10. Keep the process moving.

* You'll learn more about the behaviors listed here when you receive your *For the Common Good* 360 Assessment report.

Questions for Reflection

What am I doing to promote trust among those I work with?

What am I doing that gets in the way of promoting trust?

What am I doing to help others make progress?

What am I doing that gets in the way of others making progress?

How effectively am I engaging different voices and perspectives?

Engage Unusual Voices

Those involved in a challenge are too often the "usual voices," individuals with considerable influence with a vested interest in the status quo. One way to energize a group is to engage unusual voices, or people who have a stake in the issue but do not have formal authority.

Using the stakeholder map below, think about those currently involved in your issue and place them in the quadrant that best characterizes their level of influence and their interest or "stake" in the issue.

Those in the high stake and high influence quadrant (upper right) are typically the "usual voices," and those in the high stake and low influence quadrant (upper left) are the "unusual voices."

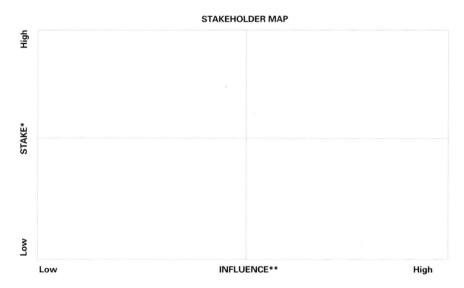

STAKEHOLDER MAP

* Stake = A person's interest in the issue; how little or how much if affects him/her.
** Influence = Tends to be perceived as synonymous with a person's position in a hierarchy.

List below additional persons or groups to include in the high stake and low influence quadrant.

Where would you place yourself in the stakeholder map and why?

Review your list of "unusual voices" above and in the upper-left quadrant of your stakeholder map. How might you engage these people so that they influence the outcome of your leadership challenge?

Working Across Factions: Start Where They Are and Speak to Their Loss

"We must do something" always solves more problems
than "something must be done."
– Author Unknown

You identified factions involved in our issue on previous pages of this section. Now, think about how to energize members of those factions by meeting people where they are on your issue, rather than where you are.

Always remember to acknowledge their possible loss.

Faction	What's their point of view?	Their possible losses?

Inspire a Collective Purpose

*I say to you today, my friends, that in spite of the difficulties
and frustrations of the moment, I still have a dream.*
– Dr. Martin Luther King, Jr.

Pause for a moment and take a few notes about your purpose for
engaging with this leadership challenge. What inspires you? Why do
you care?

Now, use the chart on the next page to generate insights about other
factions' needs and interests. Why are they involved (or not involved)?
What's driving their support, opposition or apathy? How might you begin
to develop connections between their interests and yours?

Faction	Your hypotheses about their needs and interests	Connections between their interests and yours

Create a Trustworthy Process

If you keep rephrasing the question,
it gradually becomes the answer.
– Robert Brault

Energizing others is not about gaining a majority. It's about engaging enough people across different factions in a trustworthy process. Find the balance between asking too much of people and not asking enough. Most often, you'll underestimate how much you can ask of other people.

On a scale of 1 to 10 rate your level of agreement.	1 - Strongly Disagree 10 - Strongly Agree	Why?
There is an atmosphere of trust among those involved.		
Those involved have a shared purpose.		
Those involved equally share the risks in our work together.		
There is an atmosphere of "what can we learn together?"		
Conflict is handled openly.		
We have some agreed upon next steps to move us forward.		
We've named and addressed any "us vs. them" dynamics among the group.		
There are no "unspokens" getting in the way of progress.		

What can you do to enhance the trustworthiness of the process?

What are others currently being asked to do?	What are additional things they could be asked to do?

Intervene Skillfully

To dare is to lose one's footing momentarily.
Not to dare is to lose oneself.
– Soren Kierkegaard

Leadership Behaviors

1. Articulate purpose to guide actions.

2. Make conscious choices among alternative actions.

3. Change course when actions are not leading to progress.

4. Raise uncomfortable or difficult issues that impact the group's progress.

5. Take action when needed to make progress.

6. Turn work back to those who must do the work.

7. Try different approaches to help the group make progress.

8. Continue to assess the situation while taking action.

9. Strategically use my strengths and the strengths of others to make progress.

10. Manage conflict in a constructive way.

* You'll learn more about the behaviors listed here when you receive your *For the Common Good* 360 Assessment report.

Questions for Reflection

What do I seem willing to do in order to make progress?

What do I appear to be less willing to do?

What do I tend to do when I feel "stuck"?

What could I do differently to effectively mobilize others?

Raise the Heat

If you really want to make progress, eventually you'll need to raise the heat. Review your take on the temperature and your faction map. (Pages 74 and 76)

List possible ways you could raise the heat with the factions involved with your leadership challenge.	Which faction(s) will be impacted if you raise the heat?

Who else could help you raise the heat in this way?	How risky, on a scale of 1 to 10, would this be for you?
	1 - No added risk 10 - Great risk
	1 - No added risk 10 - Great risk
	1 - No added risk 10 - Great risk
	1 - No added risk 10 - Great risk
	1 - No added risk 10 - Great risk

Hold to Purpose

You may write me down in history
With your bitter, twisted lies,
You may trod me in the very dirt
But still, like dust, I'll rise.
– Maya Angelou

Maintain your focus on what you want to accomplish. The more provocative your vision, the more others will try to distract you. Don't let them.

Using the diagram on the opposite page, mark "X" where you think an impartial observer of your time, habits and behaviors would rate how well you are holding to your purpose.

What evidence would they see to justify the ranking?

Now, using the questions below as prompts, take a moment to reorient to your purpose.

What is your leadership challenge or opportunity?

Why are you working on this?

What do you care about related to this challenge?

Intervene Skillfully

106

PURPOSE METER

HIGH

You demonstrate your commitment to purpose consistently in words and actions. Anyone could tell exactly what concerns you and why.

MEDIUM

Your focus is sometimes fuzzy. An observer would need to follow you for a day or two or inquire patiently to discover what you care about.

LOW

If someone watched you for a week, they'd see little or no evidence that this issue is important to you.

Give the Work Back

We all participate in weaving the social fabric;
we should therefore all participate in patching
the fabric when it develops holes.
– Anne C. Weisberg

Progress on adaptive challenges requires work by many, not by few.

What have you done, or are you doing, to give the work back?	What have been the results?

What else could you do to give the work back?	What do you think the results would be?	How difficult, on a scale of 1 to 10, would it be for you to do this?
		1 - Not difficult at all 10 - Extremely difficult
		1 - Not difficult at all 10 - Extremely difficult
		1 - Not difficult at all 10 - Extremely difficult
		1 - Not difficult at all 10 - Extremely difficult

Ideas you ranked as easier to accomplish may provide some "quick wins" that will motivate you to tackle more difficult work.

Speak From the Heart

Almost every wise saying has an opposite one,
no less wise, to balance it.
– Santayana

Earlier in this playbook, you answered these questions: "Why are you working on this? What do you care about related to this challenge?" Review your answer.

How often do you share your beliefs and personal stories with other stakeholders?

Are there some stakeholders with whom you haven't shared these thoughts? If so, who and why?

The key is to strike a balance and not become overly emotional or overly detached and inexpressive. Where do you fall on this continuum?

| 1 | 2 | 3 | 4 | 5 |

Overly Emotional	Appropriate Balance for Speaking from the Heart	Too Detached and Inexpressive
• You constantly let your emotions get the best of you.	• You allow yourself to speak authentically and respectfully about values.	• You never speak about values or show emotion.
• You rely solely on emotional anecdotes (oftentimes your own), rather than objective data to make your case.	• When making your case, you intersperse anecdotes and hard data with ease.	• You are not open to using qualitative or anecdotal data to support your case.
• You have trouble connecting with or inspiring anyone not already moved by your issue.	• You have developed allies who were moved by emotion and others moved by data and logic.	• Meetings feel very business-like and lack passion and energy.
		• Few people are truly inspired by your work on this challenge.

Immunity to Change

Many *For the Common Good* experiences include a process developed by Robert Kegan and Lisa Lahey. You can read more about this process in their book *Immunity to Change: How to Overcome it and Unlock the*

	1.	2.

Potential in Yourself and Your Organization. You will use the chart below as you complete your *Immunity to Change.*

3.	4.	

SECTION III

Onward!

CHAPTER EIGHT

Experiments

Experiment Log

Ideas about how to make more progress on your leadership challenge will come to you throughout your *For the Common Good* experience. Use the following pages to list these ideas — we'll call them experiments — as they emerge for you. These experiments might come out of your peer consultation activity, working with your coach or your team, from the different exercises in this book or elsewhere. We encourage you to track your experiment ideas here.

Think about the purpose of each experiment. Briefly describe what you'll do and when you'll do it. Take time to assess the risk, effort and probability of success.

Remember the purpose behind experiments is to find more data, to learn. As long as you are learning, there is no such thing as failure. Begin to develop a mindset of, "what did I learn?" rather than, "did the experiment solve the problem?"

POSSIBLE EXPERIMENT

Purpose of the experiment:

What would you actually do?

Purpose of the experiment:

What would you actually do?

Purpose of the experiment:

What would you actually do?

Purpose of the experiment:

What would you actually do?

Purpose of the experiment:

What would you actually do?

Purpose of the experiment:

What would you actually do?

How much of a stretch is this for me?	How risky is this for me?	How sure am I that I will learn something?	How much effort will it take?
Big Stretch 7 6 5 4 3 2 1 No Stretch	High Risk 7 6 5 4 3 2 1 No Risk	Absolutely Sure 7 6 5 4 3 2 1 Not at all Sure	High Effort 7 6 5 4 3 2 1 No Effort
Big Stretch 7 6 5 4 3 2 1 No Stretch	High Risk 7 6 5 4 3 2 1 No Risk	Absolutely Sure 7 6 5 4 3 2 1 Not at all Sure	High Effort 7 6 5 4 3 2 1 No Effort
Big Stretch 7 6 5 4 3 2 1 No Stretch	High Risk 7 6 5 4 3 2 1 No Risk	Absolutely Sure 7 6 5 4 3 2 1 Not at all Sure	High Effort 7 6 5 4 3 2 1 No Effort
Big Stretch 7 6 5 4 3 2 1 No Stretch	High Risk 7 6 5 4 3 2 1 No Risk	Absolutely Sure 7 6 5 4 3 2 1 Not at all Sure	High Effort 7 6 5 4 3 2 1 No Effort
Big Stretch 7 6 5 4 3 2 1 No Stretch	High Risk 7 6 5 4 3 2 1 No Risk	Absolutely Sure 7 6 5 4 3 2 1 Not at all Sure	High Effort 7 6 5 4 3 2 1 No Effort
Big Stretch 7 6 5 4 3 2 1 No Stretch	High Risk 7 6 5 4 3 2 1 No Risk	Absolutely Sure 7 6 5 4 3 2 1 Not at all Sure	High Effort 7 6 5 4 3 2 1 No Effort

POSSIBLE EXPERIMENT

Purpose of the experiment:

What would you actually do?

Purpose of the experiment:

What would you actually do?

Purpose of the experiment:

What would you actually do?

Purpose of the experiment:

What would you actually do?

Purpose of the experiment:

What would you actually do?

Purpose of the experiment:

What would you actually do?

How much of a stretch is this for me?	How risky is this for me?	How sure am I that I will learn something?	How much effort will it take?
Big Stretch 7 6 5 4 3 2 1 No Stretch	High Risk 7 6 5 4 3 2 1 No Risk	Absolutely Sure 7 6 5 4 3 2 1 Not at all Sure	High Effort 7 6 5 4 3 2 1 No Effort
Big Stretch 7 6 5 4 3 2 1 No Stretch	High Risk 7 6 5 4 3 2 1 No Risk	Absolutely Sure 7 6 5 4 3 2 1 Not at all Sure	High Effort 7 6 5 4 3 2 1 No Effort
Big Stretch 7 6 5 4 3 2 1 No Stretch	High Risk 7 6 5 4 3 2 1 No Risk	Absolutely Sure 7 6 5 4 3 2 1 Not at all Sure	High Effort 7 6 5 4 3 2 1 No Effort
Big Stretch 7 6 5 4 3 2 1 No Stretch	High Risk 7 6 5 4 3 2 1 No Risk	Absolutely Sure 7 6 5 4 3 2 1 Not at all Sure	High Effort 7 6 5 4 3 2 1 No Effort
Big Stretch 7 6 5 4 3 2 1 No Stretch	High Risk 7 6 5 4 3 2 1 No Risk	Absolutely Sure 7 6 5 4 3 2 1 Not at all Sure	High Effort 7 6 5 4 3 2 1 No Effort
Big Stretch 7 6 5 4 3 2 1 No Stretch	High Risk 7 6 5 4 3 2 1 No Risk	Absolutely Sure 7 6 5 4 3 2 1 Not at all Sure	High Effort 7 6 5 4 3 2 1 No Effort

POSSIBLE EXPERIMENT

Purpose of the experiment:

What would you actually do?

Purpose of the experiment:

What would you actually do?

Purpose of the experiment:

What would you actually do?

Purpose of the experiment:

What would you actually do?

Purpose of the experiment:

What would you actually do?

Purpose of the experiment:

What would you actually do?

How much of a stretch is this for me?	How risky is this for me?	How sure am I that I will learn something?	How much effort will it take?
Big Stretch 7 6 5 4 3 2 1 No Stretch	High Risk 7 6 5 4 3 2 1 No Risk	Absolutely Sure 7 6 5 4 3 2 1 Not at all Sure	High Effort 7 6 5 4 3 2 1 No Effort
Big Stretch 7 6 5 4 3 2 1 No Stretch	High Risk 7 6 5 4 3 2 1 No Risk	Absolutely Sure 7 6 5 4 3 2 1 Not at all Sure	High Effort 7 6 5 4 3 2 1 No Effort
Big Stretch 7 6 5 4 3 2 1 No Stretch	High Risk 7 6 5 4 3 2 1 No Risk	Absolutely Sure 7 6 5 4 3 2 1 Not at all Sure	High Effort 7 6 5 4 3 2 1 No Effort
Big Stretch 7 6 5 4 3 2 1 No Stretch	High Risk 7 6 5 4 3 2 1 No Risk	Absolutely Sure 7 6 5 4 3 2 1 Not at all Sure	High Effort 7 6 5 4 3 2 1 No Effort
Big Stretch 7 6 5 4 3 2 1 No Stretch	High Risk 7 6 5 4 3 2 1 No Risk	Absolutely Sure 7 6 5 4 3 2 1 Not at all Sure	High Effort 7 6 5 4 3 2 1 No Effort
Big Stretch 7 6 5 4 3 2 1 No Stretch	High Risk 7 6 5 4 3 2 1 No Risk	Absolutely Sure 7 6 5 4 3 2 1 Not at all Sure	High Effort 7 6 5 4 3 2 1 No Effort

Conclusion

A traditional conclusion isn't possible for this book. Only you could truly write it, because by now there is more of you in these pages than there is of us.

We trust you will develop your own closing for your *For the Common Good* experience. Some will be profoundly moved by the experience. Others will pick up some new approaches to leadership. Some might not enjoy the experience, but most attendees report it helps them exercise more leadership in their work and life.

Allow us to offer a bit of advice to consider as your initial experience comes to an end.

First, don't go it alone. The exercise of leadership is complicated and risky. Don't try to do it by yourself. Find allies and confidants. Engage others. Share the leadership. You and the efforts you care about will be better off.

Second, don't use the jargon with others. We use certain terms and phrases for the purpose of teaching and learning. Words like "raise the heat," "adaptive challenges" or "diagnose situation" might be useful in a classroom, but may or may not be useful when engaging with others. Don't turn others off with words and phrases that don't make sense to them.

Third, don't stop learning. Leadership and learning go hand in hand. You simply don't know what you don't know when working on tough — adaptive — challenges. You can't lead on tough challenges if you aren't learning.

Fourth, use the dashboard at the back of this book. It's a quick and easy way to track whether your leadership efforts are on track.

Fifth, stay in touch with the people from your program, participants, faculty and staff. Use them as confidants, allies and accountability partners.

Sixth, stay in touch with the ideas. Here are several ways to do so:

Konza Clubs

Konza Clubs ("Konza" was one of the Native American names for the land we now call Kansas) have been created in several communities to help participants continue learning with others from their community. Visit *www.kansasleadershipcenter/konzaclubs* to find the existing clubs and information about how to start a new club in your area.

Your Leadership Edge

Co-authored by Ed O'Malley and Amanda Cebula, this book breaks down the *For the Common Good* principles and competencies. With specific advice on how to do things like raise the heat, speak to loss, give the work back, etc., this book is a tremendous resource for anyone trying to put the *For the Common Good* ideas into action.

On the Balcony

On the Balcony conversations hosted by KLC president and CEO Ed O'Malley (via telephone conference call) offer an opportunity to continue exploring your new-found knowledge and skill. Visit *www.kansasleadershipcenter.org/onthebalcony* to find a schedule for upcoming calls and links to the podcasts.

The Journal

The Journal, published quarterly by the KLC Press, inspires leadership for the common good. People all over Kansas are leading on tough challenges, and *The Journal* tells their stories. Each issue of the magazine features provocative writing, photography, artwork and design and explores "big ideas" about leadership and civic life. Visit *The Journal* archive at *www.kansasleadershipcenter.org/thejournal.*

For the Common Good: Redefining Civic Leadership

Co-authored by Ed O'Malley and David Chrislip (author of *The Collaborative Leadership Fieldbook*). David and Ed tell the story behind the creation of the Kansas Leadership Center and assert that leadership in Kansas and beyond must become more purposeful, engaging and provocative if we are to make progress on our daunting challenges. Get yours via *www.amazon.com.*

For the Common Good: Workbook

Refresh your thinking with this workbook/video series. Designed to complete alone or with a group, no matter the level of exposure to the *For the Common Good* ideas. Visit *www.kansasleadershipcenter.org/ leadershipondemand* to learn more.

For the Common Good: Teaching Guide

Co-authored by Chris Green and Julia Fabris McBride. This book is great for anyone interested in our methods of instruction: Case-in-Point, case studies and coaching. (Coming soon from the KLC Press).

You'll recall we made some assumptions about your motivation in the introduction.

We assumed at some level, you believe we all share responsibility for acting together in pursuit of progress.

Through your program experience, you've learned you're not alone in that sentiment.

We trust you've gained not only tangible leadership skills to make a difference in your community, however you define it, but the intangible strength, wisdom and camaraderie that comes naturally with working and striving for the common good.

We are honored to be your partner and look forward to a long and fruitful relationship.

Onward!

Notes

Notes

Notes

Notes

Notes

Notes

Notes

Notes

Notes

Notes

Notes

Notes

Notes

Notes

Notes

Notes

Notes

Notes

Notes

Dashboard

Like a dashboard in your car, the subjective data points on this sheet are critical indicators of your leadership efforts. Consistently scoring well on these measures should translate to progress on your overall leadership challenge. Track your effort over time.

	Date: _____	Date: _____	Date: _____	Date: _____
Your level of authority or credibility with <u>all</u> the critical stakeholders	High 7 6 5 4 3 2 1 Low	High 7 6 5 4 3 2 1 Low	High 7 6 5 4 3 2 1 Low	High 7 6 5 4 3 2 1 Low
The level of disequilibrium (heat) in the organization or community	Too High! 7 6 5 4 3 2 1 Too Low	Too High! 7 6 5 4 3 2 1 Too Low	Too High! 7 6 5 4 3 2 1 Too Low	Too High! 7 6 5 4 3 2 1 Too Low
Who is doing the work?	All Necessary Stakeholders 7 6 5 4 3 2 1 Just Me!	All Necessary Stakeholders 7 6 5 4 3 2 1 Just Me!	All Necessary Stakeholders 7 6 5 4 3 2 1 Just Me!	All Necessary Stakeholders 7 6 5 4 3 2 1 Just Me!
How well do I manage my triggers?	Very Well 7 6 5 4 3 2 1 Not Well	Very Well 7 6 5 4 3 2 1 Not Well	Very Well 7 6 5 4 3 2 1 Not Well	Very Well 7 6 5 4 3 2 1 Not Well
How actively are you experimenting to advance your vision?	Several in the Last Month 7 6 5 4 3 2 1 No Recent Experiments	Several in the Last Month 7 6 5 4 3 2 1 No Recent Experiments	Several in the Last Month 7 6 5 4 3 2 1 No Recent Experiments	Several in the Last Month 7 6 5 4 3 2 1 No Recent Experiments

For the Common Good Leadership Principles and Competencies

Leadership Principles

1. Leadership is an activity, not a position.

2. Anyone can lead, anytime, anywhere.

3. It starts with you and must engage others.

4. Your purpose must be clear.

5. It's risky.

Four Competencies of Leadership

Diagnose Situation

- Explore tough interpretations
- Distinguish technical and adaptive work
- Understand the process challenges
- Test multiple interpretations and points of view
- Take the temperature
- Identify who needs to do the work

Energize Others

- Engage unusual voices
- Work across factions
- Start where they are
- Speak to loss
- Inspire a collective purpose
- Create a trustworthy process

Manage Self

- Know your strengths, vulnerabilities and triggers
- Know the story others tell about you
- Choose among competing values
- Get used to uncertainty and conflict
- Experiment beyond your comfort zone
- Take care of yourself

Intervene Skillfully

- Make conscious choices
- Raise the heat
- Give the work back
- Hold to purpose
- Speak from the heart
- Act experimentally

About the Authors

Ed O'Malley is the founding president and CEO of the Kansas Leadership Center, the home of the *For the Common Good* experiences. A former state legislator and gubernatorial aide, Ed started the Kansas Leadership Center in January 2007.

Julia Fabris McBride is the vice president of the Kansas Leadership Center and has a background in theater and executive coaching. She joined the Kansas Leadership Center in 2008.

Amy Nichols is a communications associate with the Kansas Leadership Center and first experienced these ideas as a program participant. She joined the Kansas Leadership Center in 2012.

For the Common Good: Participant Handbook is designed to be a companion for your *For the Common Good* leadership development experience. This handbook will help you prepare for your experience, engage with the ideas during your experience and thrive afterward.

About the Kansas Leadership Center

The Kansas Leadership Center, the home of *For the Common Good* experiences, was established by the Kansas Health Foundation to add significant value to the leadership development efforts undertaken by the foundation since its early days.

The Kansas Leadership Center equips people in community, business, faith, government and nonprofit sectors with skills to make positive change for the common good.

The Kansas Leadership Center is headquartered in downtown Wichita, Kansas:

325 E. Douglas Ave.
Wichita, KS 67202
www.kansasleadershipcenter.org
316.712.4950